The Courage Code

The Courage Code

IT'S YOURS. BREAK IT. OWN IT. USE IT.

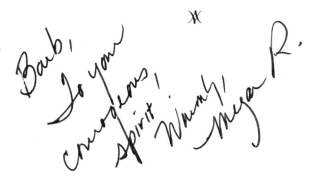

Barb,
To your courageous spirit! Warmly, Megan R.

MEGAN RAPHAEL & JENNIFER BYRON

UTOPIA PRESS
TRAVERSE CITY, MICHIGAN

Raphael, Megan.
The courage code : it's yours—break it—own it—use it /
Megan Raphael & Jennifer Byron.—1st ed.—Traverse City, Mich. :
Utopia Press, 2006.
p. ; cm.
ISBN-13: 978-0-966160-5-3
ISBN-10: 0-9661060-5-9
Contains interviews with 44 women who have redefined the meaning
of courage in their own lives.
1. Women—Identity. 2. Courage. 3. Self-realization in women.
4. Women—Life skills guides. 5. Women—Psychology.
I. Byron, Jennifer. II. Title.
HQ2037 .R37 2006
305.42—dc22 0604

Cover design by Nielsen Design Group, Inc.
Text design by Aimé Merizon

Poem on page ix from Eileen Fisher Ad Campaign 2002–2003

UTOPIA
PRESS

126 1/2 East Front Street
Traverse City, MI 49684
www.utopiapress.com

Contents

Acknowledgments vii

Introduction xi

It's Yours. Break it. 3

It's Yours. Find it. 55

It's Yours. Own it. 133

It's Yours. Use it. 205

It's Ours. Share it. 255

Afterword 313

Biographies 317

About the Authors 363

Courage Project 365

ℵ Acknowledgments

WE ARE GRATEFUL to so many people who encouraged and supported us in having the courage to bring this book into the world; this was truly a collaborative effort. Special thanks from both of us to all the women we interviewed and to the women we've worked with over the years; they opened their hearts and minds, and gave us hope. To Paul Sutherland for his deep commitment to helping us and other women find our own utopia. To Omega's Women and Power Conference for creating a new vision for ourselves. To Paolo Gianturco who breathed life into the manuscript. To Gail and Jerry Dennis who cheered us on. To our speedy transcriptionist, Lori Perz. To our cover designers extraordinare, Emily Mitchell and Tim Nielsen. To Mardi Link for her editing and marketing wisdom, and Aimé Merizon for her design and editing brillance.

Megan

I give thanks to the long line of strong women I come from who showed me a different way. To the men I've known and worked with who showed me what true equality is. To my fun, wise women friends. To Len Leritz and his sound Developmental Model. To the love of my life, Peter, for always standing beside me. To my kids, Ryan and Alex, who keep me grounded and growing. Finally, thanks to my dad, the writer.

Jennifer

My heart is filled with gratitude for the loving support of my friends and family, my project teams, and divine guidance; without which none of this would be possible. A special note of love and thanksgiving goes to Mel who always knew just what I needed.

*A woman knows life takes shape
in big and small spaces, and the moments in between.*

*When we're simply ourselves, in the everyday act of being,
we don't have to move mountains or make miracles...
but sometimes we do anyway.*

*You can see it in the many paths we take
and in how we come together to create something greater
than any one of us could alone...*

Women change the world every day.

)(

✖ Introduction

DURING OUR YEARS as consultants, teachers, trainers and coaches we've had the opportunity to meet countless women who are leading amazing lives—self-determined lives, courageous and powerful lives. Women who are making a difference in the world.

Through conversations we discovered most of these women didn't see themselves as we saw them; they didn't see their lives as particularly amazing, powerful or courageous. They felt frustrated with their lack of courage in how they lived their lives. They rarely believed their routine lives were changing the world in a meaningful way. They didn't feel their feminine wisdom and approaches were valued in the world. They were discouraged with the direction the world was going and couldn't figure out how they could impact it.

WHY?

The more we saw and heard, the more interested we became in understanding what was contributing to those feelings. Why the contrast between what we saw in the women, and what they saw in themselves? Why didn't they recognize their everyday actions as courageous, powerful, and changing the world?

We are passionate about women believing in their own power. The world needs women's abilities to relate, share, collaborate, seek solutions, give, build bridges, resolve, care, envision, understand, lift up, encourage, intuit, communicate, look out and look in. Every woman is part of a force that is changing the world, everyday, in large and small ways.

THEIR STORIES

We set out on a writing adventure with an agenda to interview women throughout the country about their self-determination, power and courage. We thought by inviting women to tell their stories they would begin to see themselves differently. By sharing their stories we knew they would inspire others as well. We chose 44 women in an intentional, although not scientific, manner and set some guidelines for the selection; we wanted a cross section of women of different ages, ethnicity, sexual orientation, and geographic areas. Our goal was to focus on "everyday" women, while also including some women who would be more easily recognized for their outward accomplishments.

While we could have chosen any number of women friends who would have fit the bill as courageous, we decided early on that we wanted to interview women we didn't know well. We began with a brainstormed list of all the women we admired for how they were living their lives, and as we asked them for names of other women, the circle widened.

You'll notice within the book we refer to our interviewees only by their first names. Hopefully, you'll get to know them as you would a friend, without the formal trappings of title, position, or even details of age and geography. Sometimes focusing on another woman's accomplishment makes our own everyday achievements seem smaller. So we invite you to learn from these women; knowing that regardless of their accomplishments, we all face everyday challenges and struggles. At the back of the book we've included the biographies of these courageous women so you can learn more about their lives.

Their stories are included at the end of each section of the book: Break It, Find It, Own It, Use It and Share It. In truth, they could have been placed in any of the chapters since all the concepts and chapters are connected. Yet, each woman's voice seems to have a special message that illustrates a chapter, guiding us to place their story in a particular order. These women had much to say about all of the book's concepts and we wanted their voices to be heard.

We listened as they detailed their struggles and triumphs in everyday life. We were moved to tears and even shrieked with laughter as they shared their stories. They discussed heady concepts while tapping deep into their hearts for truth.

Our interviews confirmed to us the power and beauty of women's courage. We are stronger now in our conviction that it is women who are and will continue to catalyze real change in the world. Sparked by their unwillingness to accept the old definitions and worn-out techniques, women are, as Barbara Marx Hubbard defines, "evolutionary pioneers" for creating greater transformation in the world.

The intent of this book is not to provide all the answers. We do not have all the answers. From the start of this book we have known our role is to question—not just in the context of our interviews, but to question the status quo, traditional views, and the old Codes. What we bring to this book is the ability to make sense out of the patterns that emerged from our questions.

The Courage Code will introduce you to our conclusions and insights from both our own lives and from what we learned during our interviews. We're also introducing 44 women who are, as you are everyday, living courageously. They are challenged everyday to create a life of meaning and authenticity. They have discovered the power of seemingly small choices that create mammoth shifts in their lives and in their worlds. Because they have dealt with their challenges head on, they have been successful on many levels and in many ways. As these women share their stories, we trust you will see yourself in their words.

It's Yours ✗ Break It

It's Yours ✗ Break It

*It is only by following your deepest instinct that you can lead a rich life, and
if you let your fear of consequence prevent you from following your deepest
instinct, then your life will be safe, expedient and thin.*

—K. BUTLER

Morse code, zip codes, uniform codes, world airport codes,
HTML codes. Our society and world are held together by
codes—codes that unite individuals, businesses, and countries
through laws, language, or symbols. Codes, whether a collection
of laws, or rules for structuring and conveying information,
instruct and guide our actions. They serve to define acceptable
ways of behaving, and allow large groups of people to share
complex information and communicate quickly and easily.

Oftentimes, codes are designed to transmit secret messages
in an obscure form that prevents others from understanding
what is being transmitted. These types of codes are usually
developed by one group that wants to keep another group from
having crucial knowledge or power. The group with the code is
able to effectively stop another group's entry into the inner circle of power and influence.

3

For eons there has been an unspoken language around courage—a Code—that is distinctly masculine. It's a Code that does not fit most of our feminine faces. It's a Code that defines courage in a singular way. It's a Code that excludes. Consequently, women's everyday courage is hardly noticed, barely understood, and rarely honored.

The Courage Code refers to the ways in which our society has traditionally defined courage—and along with it, concepts of self-determination, power, and yes, even changing the world. This old Code defines courage very narrowly, as big, bold acts of valor and victory. In this Code, the synonym for courage is bravery, especially in the face of immediate life-threatening danger. It refers to huge accomplishments, typically physical, such as mountain climbing, sky diving, or adventuring in the Australian outback.

The old Code promotes the idea that there is only one way of looking at courage, with little variation from individual to individual. This limited definition holds us to very rigid standards, thus diminishing the choices we all have.

The Courage Code, with its more masculine face, has sabotaged women's perception of themselves. Mention the word courage to women and the majority do not think it has anything to do with them. The pervasiveness of the old, male-oriented Courage Code has effectively changed our eyesight; we, as women, no longer even see acts of courage in our lives, unless we are riding the rapids of the Colorado River or leaping into the Potomac to rescue passengers from a downed plane.

Women see how the world views courage, so we say we're not courageous. We compare ourselves to the role models that are touted by the media and we feel we fall far short. As a result, we begin to believe we are not enough—not courageous or bold or valorous enough. We downplay ourselves and our actions.

The impact of this goes far beyond the despair or frustration women experience when we feel we don't quite meet the standards or the awful feeling of futility we get when we think what we do doesn't matter. The greater problem is the insidious affect it has on the world.

When we doubt and diminish ourselves, we don't allow our gifts, talents, strengths, and insights to be expressed and to flourish. When we diminish ourselves—when we tell ourselves that we're not really up to par when it comes to courage, self-determination, power and changing the world—we also end up diminishing others. We become fearful and resentful and begin to disdain others who may be living rich and fulfilled lives. Fear and resentment make it harder, if not impossible, for women to collaborate, share power, and accept others, and the world loses out.

Each of us has received messages about courage from our centers of influence—families, schools, peers, churches—that we have melded into our personal interpretation of the Courage Code. We've taken these messages to heart and merged them with the broader societal blasts we see and hear from all media. Together they form our web of beliefs about our own courage and our ability, as a woman, to impact the world. These beliefs can help or hinder us as we work to create a fulfilling, meaningful life.

A NEW CODE

A new way—a new Courage Code—is needed. The world needs women desperately. The world needs the feminine principles of wisdom, compassion and collaboration to balance the more masculine principles of action and achievement. We are needed to help bring greater balance, and tackle long-standing, complex problems of war, poverty, environmental degradation, and violence (to women and families). In essence, women are needed to create the world we all dream about.

This requires new thinking and new behavior. It requires a new Code. We believe it is women who have the ability to catalyze real change in the world by breaking the old Code and creating a new Courage Code; a Code that reflects our feminine faces. A Code that readily acknowledges and honors the beauty and power of women's everyday courage that can change the world.

Women have long known there are other ways to look at courage. We may not call it that because we say things like, "It's not really courage. It's just something I had to do." But we know there's something courageous, brave, and heart-stopping when we hear other women describe times when they've been the lone person in a group to state a dissenting opinion, made a life choice that flew in the face of everyone else's ideas, stood by their value of collaboration in a corporate culture that supported only competition, or toughed it out to take care of an ailing parent. Deep down we've understood there is beauty and power in these less-than-valorous, but still bold acts of courage. We've seen women relating, sharing, collaborating, standing up, seeking solutions, giving, building bridges, resolving, caring, envisioning, understanding, lifting up, encouraging, intuiting, communicating, looking out, looking inward; and we've known in our hearts that the feminine face of courage, while different than the prevailing, more masculine one, is amazing and valuable.

While women may be expressing courage and daring in seemingly quiet, everyday acts, we have not confronted the old

Courage Code directly, loudly. We've danced around the issue for a long time instead of challenging traditional definitions of courage.

There has been, however, a subtle, but powerful shift in cultural beliefs over recent years indicating that the old Code is beginning to crack. There is now greater emphasis in our society on spirituality, a deeper understanding of our connectedness with human beings around the globe, and a growing desire to tap into the feminine and bring greater balance to the world. Still, more work is needed.

What would it look like if we broke the old Code? The contrast is significant.

OLD COURAGE CODE	NEW COURAGE CODE
There is only one way to express courage.	There are as many ways of expressing courage as there are individuals. Each person's code is unique.
Courage is an outward, action-only expression.	Courage begins inward and then moves outward as an expression of heart and spirit.
Courage is big, bold, in your face.	Courageous acts can be seemingly small and powerful.

OLD COURAGE CODE	NEW COURAGE CODE
Courage, self-determination, and power—all are separate concepts, with no relationship to each other.	Courage, self-determination and power are all linked.
When we are self-determined, we have a clear goal and relentlessly strive to attain the goal.	Self-determination is not static; our goals can and need to change based on self-reflection.
Decisions about life should be based on logic and facts.	Decisions about life are made by tapping into intuition and logic; head and heart.
Self-determination comes from the individual standing alone.	Life is co-created with spirit and others.
Power comes from external sources.	Power comes from our authentic self.
Power is action-oriented, achievement based.	Power comes from *being* combined with *doing* to create the life we want.
Changing the world means big contributions and major sacrifices.	Changing the world comes from seemingly small, everyday acts.
The ability to change the world comes solely from what we do.	We change the world everyday by fully expressing who we are.

BREAKING THE CODE

There are three truths we need to understand to break the boundaries of the old Code:

1. The Courage Code is unique for each of us.

Your Courage Code, because it comes from your heart, is different than others—your neighbor's, your friend's. One size does not fit all and each of us can and do define it differently. That's the beauty of it. So breaking the code is to say, "This is *my* Courage Code, and I will define it so it reflects who I am and what I want."

2. Self-determination, power, and courage are connected.

The old Courage Code clearly separates them; the new Courage Code sees the links between the concepts and how they are all integrally tied together.

Self-determination is the foundation of courage. It's the "ah-ha" moment of realizing deep in your bones—to your very core—that this is your life and you have the ultimate responsibility for creating the life you want. It's understanding that, "I have choices and it's up to me, no one else can make the choices for my life."

Power comes when we fully own, accept, and honor our

authentic self. When we own our power—our authentic self, true north—we understand that our power is not more nor less than anyone else's. We can say, "I realize I *am* power and it comes from my being rather than having power as a result of some external source (money, car, house, position, etc.)."

Courage is the outward expression—the act—that comes from our heart and spirit. When we make choices from our authentic self and take action from our hearts, our courage expands. As we use it, we grow it.

3. It is all a process.

Oftentimes, as human beings, we think there's an end point to reach—a final destination to our personal growth and evolution. It is easy to believe that once we reach that point, our life will be nirvana—no problems, no turmoil, no confusion. This just isn't so. There is no final destination for self-determination, power or courage. There's only our life path, meandering here and there, that takes us to ever-deepening levels of knowledge and wisdom. We get to a new level, cruise there for a while, and then something comes up. A new dilemma, a new challenge. So, it's on to the next level—deeper and deeper, with yet another opportunity to learn something new about *It's my life,* or *I am power* or *I am courageous.*

BREAK THE CODE. CHALLENGE AND CHANGE IT.

Think about looking in the mirror everyday and saying, "This is my life. I am courageous. I am power. I am changing the world." The ramifications are tremendous. The rewards of breaking the old Code are:

EFFECTS OF OLD CODE	REWARDS OF NEW CODE
Confusion	Clarity about who we are
Limited choices	New choices and freedom for expressing ourselves fully
Sense of aloneness, and not fitting in	Deep connections with ourselves, others, and spirit
Hopelessness	New sense of what is possible
Despair, frustration	Sense of aliveness—we can be fully who we are
Self-doubt	Connection with our true self and value. We become who we are and shed what we aren't
Lack of meaning	Confidence that we are contributing everyday by being who we are

On an individual level, the more we find it, own it, use it, and share it, the more we have of it. When we find our self-determination, our core, we discover where our power comes from. When we own that we have power, we express it courageously in all facets of our life. So, courage is ever-expanding, supporting us in creating the life we've always dreamed about.

On a societal and global level, the more we fully express ourselves and our unique gifts, the more we serve the world and make a difference. So, courage, ever-expanding, spirals out supporting us in contributing to the betterment of the world.

WHERE DO WE START?

How, then, do we begin to challenge and change the old Code? We know a new Code is needed, but where do we start?

Change in our outer world starts from within. As Mahatma Gandhi said, "You must be the change you wish to see in the world." The first place to begin is by taking a look inside. Only by greater understanding of ourselves can we begin to change our Code. From there we can learn, commit to, and finally, create and honor a new Code.

Explore

Exploring starts by asking questions about what we believe

about ourselves, what we believe about our courage, and when, where, and why we have acted with courage in our lives.

Learn

Looking at patterns in our lives reveals where we are getting in our own way. This is necessary if we want to live more fully. Releasing fears and forgiving ourselves and others for those times when we haven't been as courageous as we wanted will move us closer to a new Code.

Commit

Committing to ourselves takes courage. If we want to break the old Code we must first commit to being courageous. By surrounding ourselves with like-minded individuals who support and encourage us, we will keep inching forward.

Honor

Recognizing and acknowledging ourselves and other women when we see everyday acts of courage supports the expansion of courage. We must, as women, take it upon ourselves to celebrate and honor those around us who are living the new Code.

STORIES OF BREAKING IT

We present the following stories of women who have courageously stepped outside the lines drawn for them by families, partners, cultural stereotypes, and prejudices. These are women who have defied traditional roles and stepped out of being limited by them. Not necessarily in loud, rebellious ways, but often quietly, refusing to be anything other than who they are. These women are following their hearts in making choices about careers, relationships, and parenting. They are breaking the old Code, and as a result, are forging their own personal Code.

Laura ✕ From the Rearview Mirror

A single act changed her life. And to this day Laura vividly remembers, in every fiber of her being, the empowering feeling she gained.

Her life today is very different from what it was back then; she's remarried to a great guy, has achieved success in her career, is surrounded by friends, and feels spiritually engaged. "Today, when I look back on my life, I know that then I did not have courage or power. I wouldn't change anything about my life now, but you need tools to get there and you need to be with the right people."

Just a few years ago Laura did not have the tools and she certainly did not have the right people around her. She was in an abusive relationship—together for ten years, married for six—and it was taking its toll. She believed she was who her abusive husband claimed she was. "When you hear it day in and day out that you're a nobody you can't help but believe that is exactly what you are." She says she is a person who thrives on people, relationships and bonds, and yet, for a long time she was completely isolated. Even her family was in the dark about what was happening in her marriage.

"I'm not so sure I really know what finally gave me the courage to leave. I was so tired of living for someone else, pleasing someone else, doing what someone else told me to do, and being what the person told me I was. I think I was just tired of not being a self-determined person." In a single moment she decided she'd had enough, got into her car, and drove out the driveway accompanied by the threatening yells of her husband. "When I left it was emotional, but so empowering. It was courage that I thought I could never find, but I did!"

One of Laura's greatest fears was not what her husband would do, but what others might say. She's struggled with self-doubt all her life, worrying about how people perceive her. But leaving her abusive relationship helped her stop worrying about what others thought of her and her life. "From that moment I realized I wasn't willing to spend as much time worrying about what others think. It really is only what I think that matters." Laura sees her courage in her willingness to confront her fear. "I define courage as not just overcoming fear but in really approaching and facing fear."

Laura attributes the quality of her life now to her strong vision for how she wants to be and live, and to her belief that she can achieve that vision. "I really need to believe and see myself there, whether it means I want to find someone I love or get to be the head honcho at work. I have to see myself there and believe passionately I can get there. I think if you believe this is for you it just naturally comes out in how you present yourself and what you say. It's what gives you confidence."

Her ability to stay focused on and passionate about her vision is strengthened by alone, quiet time. "Quiet time is my secret." She also surrounds herself with people who encourage and support her. "Put people in your life who allow you to do what you feel passionate about and want to do. If it means you love going to the movies, go to the movies. Don't surround yourself with people who hate to go to the movies. That is really important!"

The greatest tool she has, though, for maintaining her self-determination and courage is to go back to the memory of driving out of her driveway. "At that moment I did something incredible that I thought I could never do. I clearly remember driving away and watching him out of my rearview mirror as he stood at the door of our house warning me about the awful things that would happen to me if I left. Yet I did leave and *good* things happened! I can actually feel it in my body—the fear, and the courage I felt that day as I drove away. It reminds me I can do anything."

Karen ✗ Inside or Outside?

Sometimes it's important to work within the system. Sometimes it's critical not to. Karen has spent her life elegantly dancing between these two realms in the creation of a life that reflects her determination to live fully, gracefully and with a fair amount of raucous joy and laughter. What Karen has learned is that what is most important is to live beyond what we perceive are our limits.

Raised in a close-knit clan that included six children, Karen always felt like a bit of an outsider. Her father was an entrepreneur and her mother, a trained nurse, stayed home. "My mother was very much a feminist. She was athletic, played basketball, went off to college and even thought about leaving America to do mission work. I felt like I was raised between the mixed messages of having to [make] accomplishments in the outside world, and needing to be married and take care of a husband and family."

During her childhood in Wisconsin in the 1950s, Karen certainly wasn't alone in getting a mixed bag of societal and familial expectations. But Karen felt alone in her family because of her determination to make choices that honored her inner desires and not those of the outside world. "My older sister is very bright. In high school she was a merit scholar, she got the Betty Crocker homemaker award and she had a boyfriend. She had it all figured out that girls needed to shut up because boys don't pay attention to girls who know too much. Not me, I never figured that out. I never went underground. I kept banging my head against the wall and never shut up. Needless to say, I was always in trouble with my mostly male teachers and I never had a boyfriend until I was a senior in college. I wasn't going to settle for a guy—just for a guy's sake."

Karen knew she was carving out a new definition for herself of what it meant to be a successful woman. Although she was an A student, Karen was a maverick and a bit of a "bad girl." One day in her psychology class she blurted out that she was actually afraid of being successful. The revelation was startling even to her, but Karen used the awareness to identify her self-sabotaging behaviors and began to make changes. Even today, Karen uses affirmations to support herself in remembering that she deserves success.

Right out of college, Karen went to work at a prison. She knew her parents did not want her to work there, but it was clear that it was what she needed to do. "They wanted me to do mission work around the world—Africa or anywhere but in the prison. For me, it wasn't an option; I knew what I wanted to do."

And her job led her to Ron, a handsome, articulate administrator who just happened to be African American. He was definitely not who her parents had in mind as their son-in-law. People often say to Karen that she was courageous for falling in love with Ron. She sees it differently. "Meeting and marrying Ron was the easiest decision I made in my life—again, it was just what I needed to do. Looking back on it, I can see I did pretty much tell my whole family to kiss off." For Karen this was just another choice to live her life beyond the limits. For her family it was a bit more problematic. Although it took several years, everyone settled into acceptance and understanding. But it reinforced Karen's feelings of being an outsider in her family system.

Karen's professional life took her in the direction of entrepreneurship. She developed a successful fitness salon that focused on helping women make the connection between body, mind and spirit. When she decided to have children, she opened an on-site nursery to make her life and her clients' lives easier. Karen was determined to create a system that supported her as both mother and entrepreneur even though her own mother thought she should "get a decent job and a regular paycheck." Once again, Karen felt that because of her choices she didn't fit in.

And yet those very feelings were instrumental in helping

Karen take one of the most courageous steps of her life, a step that would change forever how she saw herself and her family.

An extended family wedding called Karen and her siblings to California. Their parents were not physically able to make the trip, so plans were made to travel without them. Since everyone but Karen lived in the same community, the rest of the family flew out together and Karen made plans to join them the following day. Before she could leave Karen received a phone call that her father's health had taken a turn for the worse. Since she was the only one not yet at the wedding, she made the decision to travel to be with her parents instead. When she arrived at the hospital and looked in her father's eyes, she knew this was serious. "My father had not been well for three years and had been talking about dying, but the rest of the family would just pooh-pooh it and tell him to not talk like that."

All alone with her parents in the hospital, Karen decided to start an honest conversation about his death. "I asked him if he wanted to go, if he wanted to leave and he said yes. I asked him what was stopping him...was he concerned about Mom? I reminded him that she has four children who live nearby and would all take care of her. And then I told him he didn't have to be stubborn and strong any longer. He could do what he wanted to do. I was really nervous, like somebody was going to kick my ass if they found out I was telling him it was ok to go. It took real courage."

As her siblings arrived at her parent's home, Karen shared what she had said and done and to her surprise they were grateful that she opened the door for a beautiful closure to their father's life. "I was able to lead and play that role because I wasn't so closely tied to the group. I think I turned the tide and they could all let him go. It felt like it was meant to be, that there was a reason why I was distant from the rest. I had four hours alone with him and was able to sit, hold his hand, and just be with him. It was a real affirmation to me that everything happens exactly as it's supposed to. Now I feel connected to my own power. I feel like I can successfully navigate the changes in my life. I feel like everything that came before was for a reason."

Deb ✕ One Step at a Time

Standing at the bottom of a staircase and gathering her courage to walk up the stairs, is a mental picture Deb carries, reminding her of where she's been and what choices she's made to get to where she is now.

Today Deb is at an exciting place in her life where finally she's giving herself "permission to explore other options and avenues for her creativity and involvement in issues that she cares about." As she reflects on the milestones marking her life so far—doing meaningful work, creating a work environment where others feel empowered, living in a gorgeous area, and having a wonderful family—she feels a deep satisfaction.

She also feels in some way a sense of wonderment that her life took the form it did. "I never anticipated owning any business or being in business at all." However, planned or not, she just celebrated twenty-five years of owning and building a thriving business. But it did not come easily or always measure up to the traditional standards applied to successful businesses.

The first ten years were the hardest. Deb and a partner started a magazine with little experience, few skills, and even less money. With a belief that "all would be okay," a background in writing, and a passion for the focus of the magazine, Deb anticipated a positive future. She didn't anticipate that her partner would leave the business to raise a family. For Deb, it was the first of many critical decision points about whether to close up or continue the business. "Going it alone was very challenging for me. It was a crisis point where I had to assess who I was and where I was going." Although money was extremely tight she knew she "couldn't walk away." She was determined to keep the magazine afloat.

During those first years, by all typical financial measurements of success—revenue, sales, etc.—the magazine was a dismal failure. She recalls moments when she would sit huddled in a corner of her apartment, thinking, *I can't tell all those people, my employees, who are working so hard, what is going on.* Deb vividly remembers several times when she stood at the bottom of the stairs going up to the magazine's offices, frightened to death, yet knowing she had to climb those stairs and tell her employees the bad news about the business's financial situation. "I had to figure out how to tell them this horrible news and yet, also how to inspire them. As I walked slowly up those stairs I kept asking myself, *how do I turn this into something that will keep everybody going forward?* By the time I got to the top of the stairs, and usually it was a long, slow climb, I knew what to say."

Through all the difficult times she was always committed to being truthful with her staff. "For me, it was about total honesty. And because of it we created a very trusting environment that allowed us to work together to finally achieve success." Deb knew, despite bankers and creditors telling her the magazine was failing, she and her staff were creating something powerful and wonderful. She refused to accept the financial criteria as the only measure of the business's value, pointing to the "incredible" work environment that existed and her belief in the role the magazine had in the community. "It was clear with each passing year that we [the magazine] were playing a significant part in helping the region deal with its ever more apparent challenges."

Her redefinition of success helped sustain her during this time. "What kept me going, too, was this enormous passion I had. I started a business not to start a business but out of this passion, and that carried me through. This passion and our belief in the value of what we were doing kept feeding off each other and supporting us."

Despite the sense of helplessness she felt at times in response to the economic pressures, she never let it stop her. She remembered her mother's message, "No one is going to do it if you don't do it," and held on to her positive expectations for the future. Today she realizes how courageous she was, "Often we hear that courage is something either you have or you don't. I don't agree. I find that for me, courage is almost an abhorrence for the feeling of helplessness. I think whatever situations you end up in you *always* have a choice, and that means you aren't helpless. Trying to do something in the face of what looks hopeless, well, *that's* courage." In looking back on those early years Deb realizes that many of her personal struggles were about finding ways to not feel helpless and instead, feel more powerful. "I now know that it all comes down to being comfortable from within. The irony is that I think I always had power; I just wasn't sure how to relay it externally. I believe I always had it internally and my great struggles were, how do I show that to the world? Once I was comfortable with that, I could develop the skills I needed."

After many years of struggling the magazine evolved into a highly successful publication. Today Deb is sought after to share her knowledge and insights with budding entrepreneurs. "I think what I bring to the table is that I am the least likely person to have gone into business and I survived." Her challenges have changed with the success of the business. "I've been successful so I guess I'm viewed as having power. So now I look at how I can turn my success into a kind of personal power so that others say. 'I've got it, too, and yeah, I can do that just like her!'"

Betty ✕ Elegant Courage

Some courage is loud, while in others it is expressed subtly, elegantly. Betty's courage has been in her quiet acceptance of and respect for others. "If you look at it in a quieter sort of way, not with flamboyance, you might say I am courageous."

With clarity and grace Betty described her rich and full life of eighty-three years. Her parents were both immigrants who came to this country as children. She had a "warm and accepting" childhood, and grew up with the feeling that she was "a person of consequence or usefulness." The respect she so often felt from her parents set the tone for how she saw herself and others. "Nobody ever tried to make me feel small, and no one was disrespectful of me; I was always treated like a person. Because I had this accepting feeling from my parents as I was growing up, I felt I was strong and it made me courageous." She made the point, however, that while not everyone has such a supportive family, "it doesn't matter what a person's past is—it *is* important to realize we are each a role model within our own current families."

Betty's family also taught her important lessons about accepting other people. "I never heard them speak ill about other people in a mean, small-minded sort of way. They might disapprove of somebody or dislike someone, but they were never small or mean about it." This affected her deeply. "I think I have a lack of judgmental feelings in my bones; I just believe so deeply that it is not right for anyone to judge anyone else." She drew from this wellspring of acceptance when displaying courage in her life. "You can be more courageous if you don't have the feeling that everyone around you is mean and going to take a small-minded attitude toward you!"

She waited until four days past her eighteenth birthday to get married. "It was war time and I felt I was going to be very important in my husband's life and him being able to do his job in the war." While she made the choice to get married rather than go to college, Betty continued to learn and grow, "As things worked out over the years I got an education. I just did it in a different way."

Betty and her husband had three children "in a clump," waited four years and then had three more children. She thrived as a mother, and put her energy into creating a loving, accepting home. Treating her children with respect was a key element in her parenting, "I realized that children need not only love, but also respect. A child has to know you respect them and it was important to me that my children felt that way, that I believed in them and supported them." In their household, dinnertime conversations included the children's ideas about family matters. "A strength in our home was the business of discussing personal and financial things within our family." Although there were rules about maintaining confidentiality about family matters, "the discussions kept the children involved in our activities."

Throughout her life Betty did a great deal of volunteer work, including a stint on a statewide Arts Council that was instrumental in the growth of the community arts movement in her state. Through her involvement and the people she met she saw the opportunities to open her children's eyes to their possibilities. "It was fun to talk about the writers and artists I met and give my children the idea that they, too, may someday meet such interesting people."

She was also attuned to and involved in the politics of the day. An early political awakening came about when a trio she was singing with was hired to sing Andrews Sisters-style at a benefit for those in her city who were leaving to fight the fascists in Spain. She later worked very hard as a volunteer for a political party in a number of different roles. During the Vietnam War years, while she supported Nixon because he was a Republican, she was very concerned about his positions regarding the war.

She was particularly disgusted with him after he reneged on his promise not to send troops into Cambodia. She acted on her strong feelings by writing letters to key local, state and national Republican leaders expressing her outrage. Finally, despite protests from fellow volunteers and friends, she courageously resigned from her political party. "It was something I would not have done unless I felt very strongly about it. Mine was a little voice, but nevertheless, for me it was an act of courage."

Her courage was never more obvious than when her eldest son died of AIDS-related cancer. This was an era when AIDS was rarely, if ever, mentioned; a time when it was only discussed behind closed doors in hushed tones. Betty decided, despite the negative reactions she was sure to receive, to include the true cause of his death in her son's obituary in her small town's local newspaper. "That was one time I really had to gather my courage together because I had never seen anybody else write that in an obituary. I felt I had to say he died of AIDS-related cancer even though there was a great deal of animosity about people with AIDS. It doesn't matter if AIDS was caused by their lifestyle; no matter what happened they are a good person."

In reflecting on courage in her life, Betty says she believes that, "Your whole life prepares you for being the kind of person who would either turn away and hide from a situation, or be the sort of person who would rush into it. I think you often have to be very courageous when you are dealing with your relationships in life. It is not all rushing into a burning building or anything like that. It is coping with life and going beyond thinking *Oh, I can't do this, this is impossible.*"

Patty ✗ Birthing a New Way

This is the story of a woman who had the courage to take a completely different path than her upbringing might have suggested.

As the second of nine children, Patty grew up in a classic baby-boom family in the 1950s. Her father traveled extensively as a salesperson and her mother was a stay-home mom. "There was a baby every year for a while and as I grew older I became very much my mother's assistant. I sort of did the domestic thing, unlike many of my siblings, and felt pretty much like a clone of my Mother." She greatly admired her mother's easygoing nature and practicality in housing, feeding and clothing their large family. And with her father on the road and a lack of extended family members, "we were all to ourselves—we were our own gang. I became so attached to my mother."

As a child Patty and her family were quite involved in the Catholic Church and she attended Catholic schools throughout her life. When it was time for college she wanted to go away, but her family's financial situation, and the need for her to continue helping out with childcare at home, resulted in her decision to attend a Catholic private school in her neighborhood. "That was my saving grace—being able to be more independent and still be involved at home."

Although her mother had, at an earlier age, wanted to go to college and had watched her own family send her brother instead, Patty never saw her mom express resentment about her lack of opportunities. She did, however, see that her mother was unsupported by the Church, and that forever changed Patty's beliefs about her right to make her own decisions. "I will never forget one day when I was twelve or thirteen I saw my mother openly crying on her way home from church. She said she had confessed to the priest that she was short with the children and he just told her that was a really bad thing to do. I was so mad and that taught me a lot about making my own decisions and not turning to authority figures to tell me what is right and what is wrong for my life and situation."

Eventually, Patty completed nursing school, left home, and married. When she became pregnant she decided she wanted to have her baby at home. "I started reading about birth because I had this concept of birth from my mother. She had all these babies and like all women at the time she just went into the hospital and had her baby; that was what people were always supposed to do. They were given drugs that made them 'lunatics' and husbands weren't allowed in the delivery room. It was shocking to me."

Through her research she discovered other, more natural alternatives including home birthing. Although women had been having babies at home for hundreds of years, the practice had lost favor with the advent of hospital maternity care. Initially, Patty could not find a physician or midwife who could or would deliver her baby at home, but she never gave up. "I tried really hard to find someone to do a home delivery but at first I couldn't find anybody. I finally found a doctor from Turkey who was willing to help me have a natural birth."

Patty's home birthing experience was so meaningful that she turned her own skills and focus to doing home deliveries, becoming a pioneer in her profession. As her work doing home births continued, her commitment to empowering and helping women increased. Talking with women and being by their side during their births made her appreciate even more the need for women to have reproductive choice. Her deep respect for women lead her to her current role as a woman's advocate for reproductive choice. "I try to make everyone feel like they are really valuable, they are precious, their body is precious and they should treat it with respect and everyone else should treat it with respect, too."

Her courage to follow her heart in encouraging and supporting women has been fueled by a number of personal tra-gedies in her family. Four of her siblings have died, including a brother with AIDS and a sister who had a postpartum stroke at thirty-five. "For me, courage is when you respond to a situation you are totally unempowered to [handle] and you are faced with the decision about what to do. You could run away. You could drink too much. You could do all kinds of things, but courage is the decision to stick with it and figure out how to do it. Courage is unique to each individual."

Other opportunities to act courageously have popped up throughout her nursing career. "Standing up to physicians has taken courage at times. I once attended a meeting with a doctor and I had a lot of trouble with a racist remark he made. It was really hard to express my concern, but I did it."

Power, she believes, has "a lot to do with how well you respond to the challenges in your life." Her commitment to working with women springs from "the way I perceive myself in the world. I see that I am part of a community and that everyone can make a difference ever so small. I won't win a Nobel Prize, but I won't feel like my life has been wasted either."

Mary W.S. ✗ Asserting Herself

There's nothing extraneous to Mary; no wasted movement, no embellishment of words, no aimless thought. What you see is what you get—direct, succinct, like "Mary Unplugged." It's not that raising six children trimmed her down to the essentials; it is more accurate to say that Mary knew if she was going to accomplish everything she wanted in her life she would have to get straight to the point.

Even as a young woman, Mary was shattering the mold that society wanted to confine her to. She attended college on a diving scholarship long before athletic parity between genders was even discussed. Graduating with a bachelor's degree in the early 1950s made Mary an enigma in her neighborhood. As a wife and new mother she made sure she always kept one foot in the employment ring. "I tell every woman I meet that the most important thing they can do for themselves is to keep working. It doesn't have to be full time—it can be a day a week, but it needs to get you out of the house and generating income of your own." During the years when Mary's family was expanding and growing that's exactly what she did. She wrote for the local newspaper and worked in several part-time capacities in business, education and social services.

When her children were old enough Mary decided to pursue her dreams of continuing her education. She did so in a rather unconventional manner. Mary enrolled in a Master's program at a major university located over 150 miles from her home. Each Sunday she would pack up and make the trip to campus, leaving her husband and children to navigate their daily lives. She had raised them to be independent and resourceful so she trusted everything would be just fine. And of course, everything was. Through this experience Mary gained new knowledge and a sense of satisfaction in following her convictions; her children benefited by having a mother who felt mentally stimulated and challenged. This legacy continues even now in her children—all grown and living fulfilling lives.

In the early 1970s, with her master's degree in hand and a fiery passion in her heart, Mary embarked on a twenty-plus-year career in training and development. She was a pioneer in bringing assertiveness classes to her hometown by teaching courses for the community college and other organizations. Single-handedly she helped thousands of women from all walks of life see their lives differently and gain new skills for asserting themselves. Today, mention the word assertiveness in her community and Mary's name comes up immediately.

Mary's commitment to herself has always been an inspiration to others, stimulating a fresh look at women's roles in family, business, and society. As her business blossomed she found herself speaking to large conventions and associations about the power of direct, assertive communication. In her spare time she was an active member of the local NOW chapter, and was instrumental in establishing a large and active resource center for abused women in her community.

Today Mary continues to break molds. Rather than sitting back and resting on her laurels, Mary, now in her 70s, is deeply involved in her community. She works part-time in her son's large specialty foods business, serving as a sort of ambassador for her town and region. She is active in political and women's organizations, and committed to building local awareness of national policies. She is still called on at times to teach business organizations about assertive communication. Woven throughout all her activities is her deep desire to have her strong voice heard. What else would you expect from a woman who has spent a lifetime coaching others to speak from their heart.

Judy ✗ Chosen by Courage

In the early 1980s Judy was part of a group of business women who met casually each month to share what was going on in their lives. Over the twelve years the group was together, they went through some pretty intense experiences (and revelations) with each other. For Judy, an intelligent woman with a keen eye for observation, her participation in The Good Old Girls Network was revelatory indeed.

"One of the things we all realized is that most of the decisions in our lives had been forced. They had been made out of some crisis state—a divorce, a job loss, or critical turn in health seemed to trigger most of our changes and transformations. I remember very clearly the point that I took control of the changes in my life and decided I would no longer simply react to circumstances, but actually begin to plan out changes. I said to myself—this is my life, I'm going to be thoughtful about the next move and create it."

At almost sixty years of age, Judy is no stranger to courage, having to face head-on her drinking problems, a debilitating bout with depression, and the news that her first husband was gay. She worked hard to truly live the serenity prayer and understand the need for both control and surrender while living in her truth.

"Courage did not come easily to me. I think I'm not that atypical. I'm a people-pleaser and I want approval. Courage for me was almost in spite of myself. I really did not want to be courageous. I didn't want to fight some of the battles that I fought. I just couldn't *not* do it. I think courage is the ability to stand up for what you believe even if you stand totally alone. It is easy to have courage when everyone is behind you. Courage requires standing up and telling your truth when the rest of the world may think you're wrong. It requires you to be true to your own integrity and your own truth. I don't think courage is something I choose. I think courage chooses me."

As a part of the first wave of women establishing their careers as a priority in their lives, Judy recalls the struggles she and her friends had understanding how power and control played out in the workplace. Although she was successful in the terms commonly used to describe achievement and had won at the ladder-climbing, Judy didn't like who she had become. She didn't like some of the effect her achievements had had on her soul.

In the early transitions from home to career, Judy believes women envisioned power as competitive and confrontational, the way men usually describe it.

"We made the mistake of believing that was power and we needed to emulate it in that form. I think women have a much higher level of power—they have the ability to nurture and empower other people to work together. We failed to bring that into the workplace as our own type of power." She doesn't berate herself or her female peers; Judy sees that the lack of female mentors and role models meant women adopted and adapted an approach from their male mentors that wasn't authentic to them. "I think we're still operating under a male model in organizations. I think what women have not yet learned is that until we create a female model for success, we are not going to change the corporate world. We're all—men and women—going to have to find a better balance, through the appreciation of our differences, not by trying to smooth them over. In the past we didn't try to be equal as women, we tried to be equal on male terms. We need to respect what women uniquely bring to the table."

And Judy brings plenty to that table. As a successful financial planner she helps women plan and prepare for the next change in their lives. She credits her ongoing quest for self-awareness, her consistent yoga practice, and her trusty journal with keeping her grounded on all levels—physical, mental, emotional, and spiritual—allowing her to tap into her authentic power. She believes it takes a tremendous amount of inner security to be very powerful, or full of power which leads to our authenticity. "I think you really become powerful when you are able to impart your authenticity to others and help them feel actualized and creative themselves." Judy's ability to live from this place of authentic power allows her to support her clients without any hidden agendas or need to prove herself. She can be truly present and allow the best financial decisions to come about effortlessly through cooperation and collaboration.

Judy describes her second husband of twenty years as, "strong, intelligent, and secure which allows him to give me the freedom to be all that I am." And that includes supporting Judy in the recent decision to have her father come live with them and be a part of this new changing family dynamic. Even so, it's been an adjustment for them all. "I think the first three months I had the same reaction as everybody else. Oh my God, my life is over. But I believe that we all choose everything in our life path as a learning experience—so if I chose this, I must want to learn! It has become one of the greatest experiences of my life. We are learning so much from each other. It brings tears to my eyes regularly at the wisdom we share. It's very funny now to find myself in 'new-mother mode' at this stage of my life. I'm finding

it is actually opening up a different part of me that is very interesting, and I'm enjoying getting to know that part of me, too."

Peggy ✕ Flying High

At age sixty-three Peggy is now living a wonderful life. "I am totally at peace and there's nothing I want for anymore." But it was not always that way. Earlier in her life she had to make a difficult decision, and an unusual one for women her age at the time.

Peggy remembers being a young child, maybe five or six, and seeing her uncle and his wife, who served in the Navy, in their magnificent uniforms. From that moment on she knew she "wanted to wear a uniform like that" and planned on enlisting when she was eighteen. However, in 1973, when she reached the magic age and went to join up, she discovered that women were not allowed to enter the military without their parent's signature if they were under twenty-one. "Of course my parents would not sign. That part of my life went away because by the time I was twenty-one I was married and a mother." The military vision never left her, though.

When Peggy was thirty-three years old, with four young children at home, she wanted to find a part-time job "just to get out of the house for a little while." She answered an ad for a weekend typist position and found that it was with the Army.

Ironically, where Peggy was living she saw helicopters flying overhead in the evenings and frequently thought, "Wouldn't it be fantastic to fly one of those helicopters?" She discovered the typist position was with the Army National Guard Unit where the helicopters she so admired were stationed.

She was told that if she wanted the job she would have to join the Army and go to basic training. Peggy was determined to work out a "deal" with her husband, and she enlisted for three years. "I was the oldest one in basic training and probably one of the first eight or nine women in the state who joined the Army National Guard. Up until that time it had been closed to women; it was a Men's Club. I was the only female in our Unit for the first eighteen years, and I got to do a lot of flying in helicopters and wear the military uniforms I so admired years ago."

Things became rocky when her initial enlistment was up after the three years. She was determined to continue flying— her husband was determined to have her put in for a discharge. Peggy told him "I'm not quitting!" and re-enlisted, "I ended up staying twenty-seven years."

To Peggy, self-determination means, "You have to want something and make it happen. I think maybe you're born with it. Possibly, for me, it was because I was the oldest of three girls and my dad never treated me like a girl. I believed just because I was a girl didn't mean I couldn't do anything I wanted. I think it's a combination of having some spirit in you and then that spirit has to be encouraged."

Throughout her life she became creative in figuring out strategies for overcoming the discrimination against women that she herself so often experienced. Earlier, when applying for jobs, Peggy found interviewers asking questions like, "Are you married and do you have children? Who is going to watch your children? Are you going to get pregnant again?" Each time she answered honestly she did not get the job. "So, the next interview I said, no, I'm not married, and no, I have no children. And guess what? I got the job." Over the years Peggy discovered the need to and value of speaking up as a way of dealing with discrimination and creating the life she wanted. "When I was younger I would be hesitant to speak up because I was afraid that I would be made fun of or it wasn't the ladylike thing to do or say. And somewhere around my mid-fifties, I noticed my hesitancy started to disappear."

Her courage in speaking up has served her well in her newest role as Commander of an American Legion Post, providing leadership to over one thousand members, mostly men. "There is a specially-designated parking spot reserved for the Commander and clearly marked by a sign. The first few times after being selected as Commander there were cars parked in my spot. I asked the group, 'Who is parking in my spot?' and was told, 'Oh, I didn't think you would be here,' to which I replied, 'It says Commander. It does not say the Commander is not going to be here today.' It took me about three or four months, but now nobody parks in my spot." Her message to other women is "Use your inner strength to go after what you want and don't be afraid."

Charlene ✕ Out of Her Head Into Her Heart

She came to it later in life, but her mission is clear; to help women understand and celebrate their unique, divine spark. Through the recognition of her own power and path, Charlene is creating a global community to support women in acknowledging their wisdom and strength. While it took several years and a major shift in careers to get her to this point, she says, "Since childhood, I always had a drive to be out there creating, speaking, and expressing myself in a way that would inspire others to self-validate. At the end of the day, we can't rely upon others to do that for us. We've got to find it within."

Charlene is very open about the courage it's taken to reach a place in her life where she is living and breathing her philosophies about the divine power of women. She experienced powerlessness early, growing up in a difficult family environment where old world cultural messages defined women's roles. Expectations were low and, like many children of post-depression parents, she was raised with limited ideas on generating abundance and securing a satisfying career. For Charlene, however, the most disturbing thing was observing the power differences in her household. "I didn't like growing up in a household where father had all the control and believed women were not equally as important as men. My mother subscribed to this idea, and I was expected to emulate that. It was a very difficult conflict for me because I felt I had tremendous potential—and I struggled with developing the confidence and a voice to get me there."

It took her many years to make meaning out of her upbringing. "It forced me to develop strength to say, 'I understand what this experience was all about. I'm not going to use this as an excuse for why I can't succeed, but why I can and why I can help other people learn that they can be in charge of their lives.' You can set your own expectations."

As a self-described "over achiever" Charlene spent a number of years in the corporate world doing research and consulting. She then launched into a prestigious, highly competitive Ph.D. program that required her to continually defend her intellectual capability. It was a very intense time professionally and personally; she had two young children, a spouse, a two-hour commute, a full course load, and absolutely no outside social life. But she was driven to complete her program, and she received her long-coveted degree.

One day, she found herself sitting in the car in a parking lot, "crying and beating my head against the steering wheel." She realized that she was terribly unhappy and didn't enjoy the work she had trained so hard for any longer. "I had been embroiled in logic, intellect, and data-driven projects for so long and I realized I was terribly out-of-balance. My intuitive nature was such a part of me, but I wasn't expressing that in my work."

What also came to Charlene at that moment was the realization that she'd been expressing the voice of others for so long, and not really developing anything creative on her own. It was a re-enactment of her childhood. "A person has to have a voice and be heard, whether it is through art, your typewriter keys, or by speaking. And for us to be complete as women, we need to develop strength to be able to speak our minds, and let our voice carry our ideas out to the world."

With this clear intention, she met an employment specialist who advised Charlene to start all over again in a different type of work. She began to reflect on all the things she loved to do. "All the years I spent studying world religions and feminist theology helped me develop my own voice and notions of the authentic self. In the parking lot that day, I began to make sense of my life and what I ought to be doing to contribute to humanity."

Moving forward, with love and forgiveness, is still a theme in her work as a way to live a positive life, filled with power. "It is still very energy intensive, to stay focused on the present. For so long, I was well defined by others and now I choose to define myself. It does take strength and discipline." But reaching a new plateau of personal power occurred when she discovered a new metaphor for the divine. "A balanced image of the Divine, in terms of a Mother Goddess and Father God image gives me perspective. It is a way to integrate balance—by knowing that the sacred feminine within is a source of personal power. And it makes attaining that empowered self-image complete because you see yourself in the face of the Divine. I think in order to live powerfully, with choice and integrity, we need to embrace our own divinity, and know we co-create our experiences and lessons for our own benefit. In that way, we can become authors of our own lives."

To this end, she has devoted her life to supporting women who want to feel positive and powerful. She encourages them to know themselves from a fundamental, spiritual level. "In minutia-filled, everyday life you can push through the superfluous and expand into new territory by realizing you are an individual spark of divine power. That is what you are—a spark of the God and the Goddess. When we don't view our lives that way we diminish our own capabilities."

It's Yours ⚹ Find It

It's Yours ✕ Find It

I read and walked for miles at night along the beach ... searching endlessly for someone wonderful who would step out of the darkness and change my life. It never crossed my mind that that person could be me.

—A. QUINDLEN

LIKE SO MANY THINGS in life, discovering who you are and living it, is a paradox. On one hand, it's blazingly simple: This is your life and it's up to you to choose how you want to live it. And yet, as we explored the issue with our women interviewees, and in our own lives, self-determination is surprisingly complex.

It's clear to us that self-determination is the basic, fundamental foundation underlying courage. The truth is, without believing that *this is my life and I have the responsibility to make choices that fit for my life,* courage is impossible. These core beliefs are the source of all personal expression; without them our lives will not reflect who we truly are. If a woman wants to live a life of greater fulfillment she must believe at a very deep level that she is responsible for creating that life.

We are all born with self-determination and the drive for self-expression. Think about infants; there is no holding them back from telling us, in their own way, what they want. Some of the women we interviewed said they felt self-determination was always with them and always a part of their life. They saw that from a very early age they were clearly guided by the realization that it was important for them to make decisions based on what they wanted and not what others dictated. They somehow knew instinctively, deep in their bones, that their life, and what happened in it, was up to them.

Many of the other women, however, said this was not necessarily true for them. At different points throughout their lives they had turned control and responsibility for their life over to others. They described situations where they found themselves constrained or controlled by others—parents, partners, employers. At times they saw themselves engaged in self-destructive behaviors which, in retrospect, they understood was a result of losing sight of taking responsibility for their own life. For these women, the shift away from allowing themselves to be victims to rediscovering their self-determination came later in life. Their life stories reinforced our belief that self-determination— finding our own Courage Code—is possible at any point in our lives.

Do women struggle with self-determination more than men do? In her book, *The 12 Secrets of Highly Creative Women,* author Gail McMeekin says, "I've always sensed the presence of an unconscious, deep awareness of the danger of self-expression for women. After all, our female ancestors were burned and murdered for their intuitive, creative, healing powers. I do believe that we women have a shared legacy about becoming too influential and then being attacked." Combined with this unconscious collective anxiety women may experience are the individual messages each of us have received throughout our lives about self-expression: *Be a good girl. Children should be seen and not heard. Don't be too full of yourself. Don't worry your pretty little head about it. Don't be so selfish. There's no "I" in team.* The combination can be deadly to our hearts and our minds.

It was interesting to find that the women we interviewed were far more at ease talking about their self-determination than they were about their power and courage. When asked to cite examples of their self-determination they were quick to talk about the ways in which it has shown up in their lives, even as young girls. They did not seem at all embarrassed at our description of them as "a woman living a life of self-determination"; unlike their reluctance in our conversations to be tagged as courageous or powerful. In fact, their self-determination appeared to be a great source of pride for the majority of the women we interviewed.

While it was not difficult at all for these women to describe their acts of self-determination, most of them were reluctant to take full credit for setting the course for their lives. The majority of women spoke about working in partnership with a power defined by them in different ways, including the Universe, Spirit, Creator, Goddess and God. No matter the definition, the notion was the same: While they believed strongly that it was their life and they needed to make decisions that were right for them, they saw themselves as co-creators in manifesting their dreams.

THE OLD CODE

The traditional picture of self-determination is of an achievement-oriented individual moving forward unceasingly toward a goal. Most often this person is standing alone in their resolve to achieve and accomplish, willing to knock down any barrier, never letting anything stand in their way.

In fact, the dictionary defines determined as, "move in a straight line, to decide through reasoning, fixed, limit, boundaries." Merriam-Webster's definition for self-determined reinforces this notion even further: "determined by oneself." These definitions do not reflect the feminine face of self-determination.

The old Code implies that when we are self-determined nothing outside ourselves or our own goals exists. We make decisions on our own, with little consideration of their impact on anyone or anything else, in a lincar fashion, entirely based on logical reasoning. Furthermore, once a determination is made, the goal we set is static and unchanging. Certainly, there's a grain of truth in this Code; when we act with self-determination we do make decisions based on what is right for our life, not on what others want. But beyond that similarity the culturally-accepted picture is very different from the new Code being defined by women today.

Shifting to a new Code means we need to look closer at the old Code to understand and challenge what it's really saying. There are four destructive components that make up the old Code:

1. Old Code: Stand Alone

The old Code says that when we are self-determined nothing should exist outside ourselves or our own goals. We stand alone in our self-determination with little consideration of the impact of our decisions on anyone else.

We are a culture that was founded on rebellious individualism, and we continue to pride ourselves on being a country of strong, tough, single-minded individuals. Our society is deeply steeped in and enamored with the Lone Ranger image striking out alone to conquer the wilds, overcoming every barrier with solitary steadfastness.

While this image may be appealing to some, it's downright inaccurate—he relied on Tonto to survive in the wilderness—and it is very detrimental. As Reverend Kathleen McTigue states in her article, "Wave Goodbye to the Lone Ranger,"

> While the Lone Ranger was just a character in a long-outdated TV show there are parallels between that fictional character and our own country's behavior in the international community. We speak and act as though other nations were our sidekicks or followers, with nothing to offer us but their admiration. We seem sure of where the line divides the good guys from the bad guys, and we think we know how to deal with the bad guys, no matter what anyone else might say. We ourselves are never the bad guys, no matter what suffering might come from our actions. We ride off into the sunset and rarely look back to find out how the story ends, as the dust from our action finally settles.

This individualistic thinking simply does not lead to sound choices for a country or an individual.

Self-determination does not mean, as the current Code suggests, that our choices are solely determined by oneself. Certainly a significant part of the process is solitary, and what is best for our lives needs to be determined, ultimately, by each of us, alone. However, it is a fallacy that our life direction and path is determined only by ourselves.

We are not solitary creatures and we don't live in a vacuum. We live with families, co-workers, and other human beings. We are not alone in this world. As retired Supreme Court Justice Sandra Day O'Connor says, "We don't accomplish anything in this world alone...and whatever happens is the result of the whole tapestry of one's life and all the weavings of individual threads from one to another that creates something."

2. Old Code: Use Linear Logic

The old Code says that when we are self-determined we make decisions on our own in a linear fashion, based solely on logical reasoning.

Moving forward in a self-determined way is rarely a linear process. It is a circular process that moves from assessing and considering information to taking action to reflecting and reassessing the information and taking action again, based on the new information. Certainly, assessing our information and options can create linear momentum in achieving our dreams. But we sabotage our success if we never circle back to reflect and reevaluate both our progress and our goals.

Women we interviewed talked often about how important their self-reflection and reassessment were in reaching their dreams. Sometimes out of self-doubt, but always from a desire to make sure they are on the right path, they revisited their dreams, goals, and choices. They spoke about the deeper understanding they gained about their life's meaning and purpose from self-reflection, spurring them on to even greater action.

In the old Code, action is all important. The high value the old Code places on doing and achieving devalues being and reflection. And yet, without both, we lose out. The combination of feminine principles of being, receiving, and inner knowing with masculine principles of acting and doing is a potent blend.

The value placed on logic in our society has gone way over the top. "Just give me the facts!" seems to be the mantra of the day. With our heavy reliance on rational thinking, though, we are stuck with solutions that are often shortsighted, short-term, and short on real change. Real solutions to complex problems involve understanding all factors at play—the tangible as well as the intangible. Good decision making on a personal, organizational or cultural level requires big-picture thinking and taking into consideration all information, including feelings and emotions. Not tapping into and appreciating the value of intuition undermines us as women, and results in poor decisions for all of us.

Certainly women are not the sole keepers of intuition. Women typically have an easier time, however, and are more skilled at accessing their intuition. In addition, they are more often highly attuned to the emotions and feelings in any given situation.

Whether expressed by a man or woman, all too often our culture devalues intuition and the awareness of underlying, unexpressed human dynamics. As a result, women downplay what they intuit if they cannot back it up with hard facts. Out of fear of not being taken seriously, it's the rare woman who will bravely proclaim in a business problem-solving session, "Wait, I have a gut feeling..."

And yet, as Connie Glaser, author of *Swim with the Dolphins*, says, "We often make better decisions with snap judgments then we do with volumes of analysis. The trick is in learning to trust your sense of intuition as decisions made very quickly can be every bit as good as decisions made cautiously."

Time and time again, the women we spoke with described the depth and beauty of their intuition, and how essential it has

been to them in making great decisions, personally or professionally. Their ability to live a self-determined life is directly
linked to the strength of the connection with their inner wisdom
and intuition.

3. Old Code: Stay the Course

The old Code says that decisions are static and unchanging, and
once we take action, we must stay the course, no matter what.

Too often we hear about the extraordinary individuals who,
early on, set a goal and are never swayed from that path. Goals
are great and necessary, and for some, this unflagging approach
works. However, holding these folks up as our only ideal diminishes the value of self-examination and flexibility. It also diminishes women's changing lives and changing needs.

The leadership in this country reinforces the view that once
decisions are made it is the strong leader who "sticks to their
guns" and does not veer from the path they have set, despite
new information. This unwavering resolve and unwillingness to
reconsider actions once we've made a decision is dysfunctional
and dangerous.

We frequently hear women express frustration with what
they see as their wishy-washiness. At some point in their life
they've set a goal, only to find later that this goal no longer has

meaning for them or makes sense. But because cultural norms reinforce the values of constancy and steadfastness in achieving goals, women beat themselves up for not setting a course and sticking with it, no matter what.

There are very few static decisions to be made in this life. When we buy into this cultural norm we do ourselves a huge disfavor. Even the publisher Harlequin, best known for their somewhat steamy, bodice-ripper romance novels, understands and is beginning to market this idea. Their new line of books, called The Next Novel, is designed for women "facing up to the glorious unpredictability of life."

Our choices are based only on information that is available in a moment of time. As our awareness increases, new options appear and we have the opportunity to make new choices based on this new information. Changing our minds based on new information is good—and essential for change, transformation and innovation.

THE CORE OF SELF-DETERMINATION

Self-determination is the foundation for courage and is the combination of three core beliefs. These serve as the starting place for any woman wanting a life of greater fulfillment, meaning, and connection.

1. This is MY life!

The belief that you are responsible for creating the kind of life you want.

2. I have options.

The belief that you have choices.

3. It's up to me to choose.

The belief that the choice is up to you; *you* must choose.

Taking responsibility for one's life is the main theme of self-determination. But as several women mentioned, this is not the usual heavy guilt-making type of responsibility. Each of us is responsible for looking at our situation, considering all of our options, and then trying to work through deciding what's the best thing to do at the time. This requires awareness and choice.

Awareness

Awareness is an essential part of self-determination. It is only through being conscious that we gain understanding about our desires, needs, wants and options as a way to determine the best course of action for ourselves. Sometimes this information is surprising, disturbing or distressing, for as Lillian Hellman, the famous actress once said, "It's a sad day when you find out that it's NOT accident or time or fortune, but just yourself that kept things from you." Yet, often the awareness is thrilling and exciting such as the times when we have a new insight about a longstanding issue or get a glimmer of a strength within us that we haven't appreciated before. Awareness is always fruitful.

Traditional cultural norms reinforce the value of paying close attention to, and relying on external standards defined by society, family, employer, talk show hosts, religious leaders, etc. for making our life decisions. In our celebrity-worshipping society, we are often overly-aware of and seeking the wealth, status, and lifestyles pictured in *People* and *Us* magazines. Focusing on these external standards causes us to compare ourselves to others, triggering competition, keeping score, denying our own needs and wants, seeking approval, insisting on going it alone, and/or always trying to prove our value. Every one of the women we interviewed realized that setting a course for their life based on others' definitions or expectations resulted in disconnection, dissatisfaction, and discontent.

When we become aware of and turn to our own inner guidance, self-determination looks very different. Wading through all the external messages that tell us how to be "good" or "successful" or "responsible" or "beautiful" is a daunting task, eased only by going within and listening to what's important to us. Each of us has an authentic self, a true north, that can guide us in making choices for our higher good. The majority of women we interviewed talked about the life-changing moments that came from tapping into their true north. Many spoke eloquently about times in their lives when they experienced deep depression that was only relieved when they began to be aware of their inner self. We heard over and over again from our interviewees that they found their courage only when they listened to the quiet, still voice inside. Awareness of what is important based on what we know to be true for ourselves allows us to make intentional choices for creating the life we want.

Choice

When we act with self-determination we *choose.* The fundamental choice we make is to believe *this is my life.* Then, we choose whether or not we will respect and honor that belief, and whether we will live from the place of self-determination in all areas of our life.

As our women interviewees revealed, these are choices that continually need to be revisited throughout life. Each situation we encounter—every moment of every day—hands us yet another opportunity to make the choice for how we want to live our lives. A choice whether we want to live a self-determined life or not. We choose to speak up even though our stomach is in knots, or we choose to stay quiet. We choose to tackle a problem directly, or we choose to avoid the issue even though sweeping it under the rug makes things worse. We choose to negotiate with family members about our wants and needs so we feel greater fulfillment, or we choose to stuff our feelings and deny our needs. We choose to stand up in a meeting and respectfully voice our concerns, or we silence our voice.

The feelings we get when we are making choices from our authentic self, our true north, are very different than when we are not. Some women we spoke with described a lightness in their step, a flutter of excitement in their stomach, an easing in their body. Others said they felt a knowing deep in their bones. Even if the choice was a difficult one with an uncertain result, they knew when a decision was right for them. Across the board, women referred over and over again to a gut feeling: a sense or intuition they were moving in the right direction.

Every woman expressed deep pride when she made a choice, easy or tough, that was an expression of something deep within her. Each time she acted in a self-determined way it strengthened her "true north muscle," i.e., her ability to make even tougher decisions and choices later on.

Once our women interviewees came to grips with the fact that it was up to them to create the life they wanted, the choices from there on were, in many ways, no-brainers. The awareness of their responsibility in crafting their life became a part of their very being and, at some level, it guided all their further actions. Once they made the commitment to self-determination, it became a way of life for them. And once they experienced the joy and release from finally saying and doing what they wanted and meeting their needs, they never looked back.

However, they also described their angst and trepidation when making a difficult decision or tackling an interpersonal problem. As is true for many of us, not wanting to hurt someone else's feelings was a major driver for our women interviewees. The "disease to please," i.e., the burning desire to be liked and accepted, complicated their choice-making. But the commitment to live a self-determined life made it nearly impossible to back away from tough decisions, no matter how difficult the choice was.

WHAT GETS IN OUR WAY

There are several barriers women create that sabotage and undermine our success at living a self-determined life.

1. Wanting to Be Taken Care Of

Women have come a long way in realizing we are responsible for the life we create, and having the opportunities and freedom to do what we want. We interviewed a number of First Wavers, i.e., women 60+ years of age who were the real pioneers in the world of women seeking self-expression and identities outside marriage and family. These are women who were often in their 20s and 30s before they even heard of other women who felt the same yearnings to fulfill a purpose other than being a wife and mother. It took real courage for these women to set a course for their own life when they envisioned something beyond the constraints of society's definitions.

This has changed dramatically and is continuing to shift. Younger women, more accustomed to hearing messages about their need and right to be more self-reliant, and armed with education and opportunities to make their mark, fully expect to live a life of their choosing. They have learned to identify what they want and are more skilled at communicating their needs, and creating opportunities for self-fulfillment.

However, we still hear women of all ages expressing a bit of wistfulness when they realize they must take charge of their life. There's a seed of yearning for someone in their life, usually a man, who will make their life easier. Of course, it's not very politically correct in many circles for a woman to admit that lurking somewhere in her consciousness is a desire for a sugar daddy, but the wish to be taken care of exists, nonetheless.

This desire to be taken care of undermines our self-determination for it turns the responsibility for our life over to someone else. Certainly having a partner to help share life's ups and downs is a reasonable and beautiful thing; it is when we are willing to subvert our own needs in exchange for an easing of our daily pressures and responsibilities that we lose ourselves. It truly becomes a deal made with the proverbial devil.

What is needed is another way to look at relationships; that within a healthy partnership, personally or professionally, all people can have their needs met. Each individual can create a life they want, enhancing, not threatening, the other person's self-expression. Together, as whole people, couples and families can come together in supporting each other's life purpose.

2. Believing Choices Are Limited by the "Bad Hand I Was Dealt"

It's true, many people did get dealt a bad hand. People all over the world are born into abusive, poverty-ridden, dismal situations. We need to appreciate how difficult it is to maintain an optimistic spirit and belief in a positive future in these situations. The last thing we want to do is take on the typically

American perspective that individuals who are struggling financially, physically, emotionally or mentally, could be our next president if only they'd "pull themselves up by their own bootstraps." It is much too easy for people of means, who have grown up with someone supportive in their lives, had opportunities for education, who are the "right" gender or sexual orientation, or have the "right" color of skin to play the blame game. Too often, in this country, when we reach a certain socio-economic level we begin to lose sight of our shared humanity. We feel not only disconnected from others who are different from us, but judgmental. We lose our compassion.

So, this is not a simplistic "Buck up!" answer to the very real and difficult situations that women find themselves in. We know that there are unjust, systemic problems in the world that contribute to women's high rates of poverty and violence. And we also know it's very hard, if not impossible, to overcome the odds of escaping a bad upbringing, situation, or relationship, if the focus is only on the bad hand.

Our women interviewees revealed many situations that made our hair stand up or brought tears to our eyes. As different as their situations were, however, the women still shared a common perspective. They were unwilling to remain a victim of their circumstances and they saw it was their responsibility—

and joy—to create a new vision and seek new choices for their life.

For these women, what helped them move forward was reconnecting with the voice deep inside them that reminded them they deserved a better life. They began to believe somewhere in their heart and mind that it was possible to live a different kind of life than they had inherited or created. Once they decided to focus on the satisfying life they believed they deserved, and created a new picture for their life based on what they wanted, not what they didn't want, they were able to take charge of their lives. Their self-determination made it possible for them to leave abusive relationships, change jobs, overcome addictions, begin to exercise, or speak up.

3. Seeing Few Options

The mindset that *I do not have a choice* assumes that no options exist, and therefore we must resign ourself to the current situation. If we believe in a lack of choices or no options, our fate is sealed—we will be blind to what is available.

The belief *I have no other choice!* assumes things will never be different or get any better. Given the experience of the women we interviewed there could not be a more erroneous perception. Time after time women vividly described moments in the past when their life changed dramatically, sometimes so much so that they often could not recognize the person they used to be compared to who they are now. Their past thinking, behavior, and results were 180 degrees away from their life today. Tales from their past included marital abuse, violence, depression, bankruptcy, alcoholism, and drug addiction; all light years away from the joy, satisfaction, financial abundance, healthy relationships, and physical well-being they are now experiencing.

There is no question about the resiliency of human beings, and as women, our flexibility and adaptability are legendary. No woman needs to accept her current situation unless she wants to; no matter where her choices have taken her up to now the possibilities for change and growth are unlimited.

4. Not Connecting with Our Authenticity

Often our choices do not come from our true north and we find ourselves in situations entirely wrong for us. We know our choices are not coming from our inner, authentic self when we are in situations or relationships that squash our dreams or put us in danger. We may feel desperately unhappy or completely "robotic," dead, cut off from any feeling at all.

Our women interviewees discussed what often got in their

way to living a self-determined life: lack of alone time, lack of quiet time, constant internal chatter and negative self-talk, and over-focusing on parenting responsibilities, to-do lists, household chores, and/or job demands. Each woman found specific strategies that helped her feel more relaxed and more in touch with her authentic self. Examples included carving out time for daily walking, journaling, meditation, yoga, jogging, and prayer.

Yet, even knowing how important this self-care is in their lives, the women found it difficult to sustain the discipline and energy on a regular basis. They were honest in describing times they allowed their daily responsibilities (job, family, etc.) to take precedence over quiet, alone time, even though they were aware of the consequences.

They admitted that sometimes they wanted to simply avoid listening to what their inner voice was saying. They knew exactly what the best choice was for them and yet backed away from that choice out of fear—fear of failure, fear of success, fear of not being liked, fear of being alone, fear of disapproval, fear of not being seen as competent, or fear of becoming a bag lady on the street. The times they gave into these fears took them far away from their authenticity.

To create the life we want, we must recognize when we are

truly connected with our authentic self. Discernment—the ability to identify what's true and real for us—is a learned skill. When we decide that we want to live a more self-determined and courageous life, and become aware of our choices, it is essential we discern what is truly going on within us—emotionally, mentally, spiritually, and physically. Greater awareness leads to better discernment, and therefore, more choices.

5. Forgetting Self-Determination Is a Process

We, as women, trip ourselves up sometimes by engaging in the fantasy thinking that once we have made the fundamental decision *This is my life!*, our path from here on will be smooth. We know from our women interviewees and what we know to be true from our own lives, nothing is further from the truth. We set ourselves up for disappointment and failure when we get hooked into believing that once we find our self-determination —once we get that part down—we won't experience any challenges to it ever again. We forget that self awareness is a process much like peeling an onion; each new situation that arises creates new opportunities for deepening our learning about taking responsibility for our life.

The media does not do us any favors when it comes to showing how change happens. Every message we get about change reinforces that it is not only rapid, but everlasting. Television shows solve complex personal problems in half an hour or less, and heavy-duty, long-lasting stains are removed in under a minute. We are a fast-food culture, expecting everything to happen not only in very short order, but also at our command and to our exact specifications. This is not reality when it comes to human change, and it certainly does not fit women's self-determination.

As demonstrated by the women we spoke with, our willingness and ability to act with self-determination waxes and wanes throughout our lives. At times we are crystal clear on what we want and we make the choice and take the action we needed to make it happen in our lives. Other times clarity and conviction are replaced by confusion and indecision. And even though we believe it is our life and up to us to create it, we find ourselves in situations and relationships that are not life-enhancing. The women we interviewed currently all lead very self-determined lives. However, most described abusive relationships and unhappy marriages they had once been in, previous jobs that had drained them of self-esteem and energy, and times of desperation and depression. And while these experiences were unhealthy at best, each woman learned something enriching from them. Some realized how strong they were, or it affirmed who they could count on, or they gained insights about behaviors to change. The majority of interviewees talked candidly about the wake-up call they got from these experiences; for each it was yet another "ah-ha" moment that reminded them it was their life to create.

These ongoing ah-ha moments provide the understanding that self-determination flows fluidly throughout a lifetime—sometimes smoothly, sometimes not. Change is continuous, with new decisions opening up options that were once invisible. It does all of us a disservice to believe that once self-determined, always self-determined. Or the reverse—never self-determined, well then, never-ever self-determined.

Unlike our societal fascination with the quick fix, for the majority of women the process of making new choices certainly did not happen overnight. Sometimes their decision came in an instant—we call it a BFO (blinding flash of the obvious)—as a sudden insight. But more often than not, it took women quite a while to wade through the layers of information, feelings, fears, and assumptions to really find out what was true. They described the weeks, months or years that often passed before clarity dawned and they took action.

To hold ourselves up to some unrealistic, superwoman standard is self-defeating. That is why Oprah is revered by so many women in our country. She is real about women's lives; she understands and supports women in incremental, long-term change for creating their dreams. She, like the women we spoke with, understands that making self-determined choices is an up and down process over a lifetime.

6. Getting Caught in Scarcity Thinking

Essentially, there are really only two ways of viewing the world—from a place of scarcity or a place of abundance.

Scarcity thinking is believing that our resources are limited—there is not enough to go around. There is not enough money, time, opportunities, love, clients—you name it, there just is not enough. If we believe there is not enough to go around then it follows that we view other people as greedy and threatening to us as they, too, are in competition for scarce resources. If we see that others are greedy then we believe we must eke out whatever resources are available to us in whatever fashion we can think of.

Scarcity thinking moves us away from taking responsibility for our lives. It is fear-based. We keep score, make excuses, or shift the blame. We accommodate or acquiesce to others' needs and deny our feelings. We set aside our dreams for the sake of keeping the peace or being liked, or gossip in hopes that someone else will handle the conflict. We go it alone or do not seek feedback or resources that could help us. All these behaviors are expressions of scarcity thinking.

What is very important to understand is that the underlying belief of *There is not enough* is really *I am not enough*—I am not smart enough, beautiful enough, creative enough, generous enough, and on and on.

While scarcity thinking is certainly not gender-based, for a number of reasons women are more prone to quickly jump to *I am not enough.* Throughout history in all parts of the globe, women have been told in obvious, and not-so-obvious ways, they don't count, that they are not enough. Look at the countless structures and systems that do not consider or support women; examine the pictures of gatherings of world leaders and you will see a lack of woman leaders sitting at the same table. Combine this with the different ways we are encouraged to compare ourselves to others and hold ourselves to nearly impossible standards. From supermodels to the larger than life "I-can-run-a-Fortune 500-company-while-cooking-a-gourmet-meal-with-my-nursing-baby-in-my-arms," women get the message: You are not enough. No wonder women flip into scarcity thinking at a moment's notice.

The danger to scarcity *I am not enough/there is not enough* thinking is not only the undue pressure and guilt it creates, but how far it takes us away from our authentic self. And when we shift out of our true north and away from our authentic self, our choices become more limited and we do not get the results we want. We end up getting stuck in lives that are meaningless and do not reflect our gifts. We keep ourselves small.

THERE IS ANOTHER CHOICE

The other choice we have is abundance thinking. Unlike scarcity thinking, with abundance thinking we see there are enough resources for us and for everyone, and we view other people as having needs versus being greedy. We understand that how we choose to allocate or use resources is what's important—whether we are talking about time, money, business, energy or love. And of course, the fundamental difference is the underlying core belief, *I am enough!*

Abundance thinking is not fear-based. It keeps us operating from our authentic self, and expands our options. Abundance thinking allows us to build safe, respectful, resolved relationships, and move forward towards achieving our dreams and goals. If we want to create a satisfying, meaningful life, only abundance thinking will take us there.

The differences are astounding in the choices and behaviors

that spring from abundance thinking versus scarcity thinking. When we believe we are enough we can trust our abilities to solve problems and make our dreams come true. When we see there are enough resources to go around and that all people have needs we can share power, collaborate, listen, understand, be inclusive, ask for input, and negotiate with others. And because we are in touch with and accept ourselves we can also allow others the same freedom in living their own self-determined life.

To free ourselves from scarcity thinking means we must recognize and understand when and why we shift out of abundance thinking. We may start our day and/or find ourselves during the day coming from a place of abundance. We feel great; calm, relaxed, expansive. And then, wham! Something happens—a conversation, an event, a comment—that triggers us into scarcity thinking. Suddenly we find ourselves impatient, defensive, competitive, or disappearing literally or figuratively. Immediately our ability to see and think through our options is shut down; our willingness to take responsibility for our actions has gone out the window.

There are three factors that can flip us out of abundance thinking into scarcity thinking: 1) When we feel tired, 2) When we feel stressed, or, 3) When we feel threatened. Experiencing any of these conditions means it is much more likely that we move into or get stuck in scarcity thinking and behavior.

It is far easier to operate from abundance thinking when we are relaxed, well-rested and feeling safe. The world looks a whole lot better after a good night's sleep, a vacation, or even a brief time alone. As women interviewees shared, their lives changed and improved when they understood this link, and started taking better care of themselves. They intentionally began making changes, small and large, to their lives that helped them feel more rested, relaxed and safe. Whether it was through more alone time, getting a massage, walking the beach, exercising, rearranging work and home life for greater flexibility and less stress, cutting back on watching the news, or surrounding themselves with positive people, the impact was the same. They saw the world and their possibilities differently. Over and over again women told us that taking care of themselves, emotionally, mentally, spiritually and physically, made them see the "sky was the limit!" The number and quality of their options and choices expanded in direct relationship to how their energy and optimism expanded.

We can choose between scarcity thinking and abundance thinking. No matter how we have previously viewed life, we can, through awareness and choice, create new possibilities.

A NEW CODE

The women we spoke with are redefining self-determination—living a new Code—in quiet and loud ways. While each has crafted a life that reflects their own unique choices, there are several common themes to the new Codes:

1. Self-determination is always within our reach.

Acts of self-determination often surprise us and happen despite our fears or our belief that we lack courage to make the choice. Sometimes it takes a while to muster up the courage to act in a self-determined way. Self-determination is a process that continues throughout our lifetime, and it's always possible, in the small and large choices we make in the moment, to overcome self-doubt and self-sabotage, and shift into self-determination.

2. We have ever-expanding choices available to us.

Each day, each moment, presents new choices based on new information we discover about ourselves and our world. We always have the choice to dig deep to find out more about who we truly are and what we want. And we always have the choice to make decisions that allow us to live more fully and authentically. Our choices are never limited, but always expanding.

3. We are surrounded by unlimited resources.

As we create a self-determined life we have abundant resources to assist us. We have incredible inner resources—knowing what's important to us, what we truly want and need for the kind of life we want to live, our ability to sort through and make sense of complex information, and our intuition and inner knowing. We are also surrounded by others' ideas, tools and friendship to help us create our dreams and expand our perspective. For many women an important resource is their personal relationship with a higher power, in all the many ways women describe it—Universe, Creator, Goddess, God, and so on. Tapping into our spirituality can give us a greater understanding of the "gifts" we have to serve the world and a deep sense of a co-creative partnership.

4. As we become more self-determined, we come more fully into our power and courage.

Self-determination is clearly the foundation of our power and courage; the first step along the way to living fully and richly. Deepening our knowledge and understanding of who we truly are sets us on a path of owning our power and using our courage in ways that change the world.

STORIES OF FINDING IT

We now present women who made the decision to live authentically and fully. Even when feeling trapped in difficult situations or blind-sided by a life crisis, they dug deep to find their self-determination. They faced life head on with quiet, fierce courage. These are the stories of women who found their own Courage Code and transformed their lives.

Robin ✗ Tales from a Summer Vacation

A psychiatric unit is a strange place to find oneself. For Robin, who found herself in a psych ward one summer, it was the beginning of self-discovery and renewal.

Robin had a tough year leading up to what she calls her breakdown. Her much-loved grandfather died, she and her husband moved to a new area, and she was working in a position that she "was not cut out for." Because of a lack of time and energy she had not made many new friends. Add to the mix a new pregnancy that threw her chemical balance out of whack and she was quickly running into trouble. "I started having severe panic attacks and anxiety." After a few weeks of trying alternative treatments such as hypnosis and herbal supplements she became suicidal and realized that more intensive care was necessary. Robin committed herself to the psychiatric unit of a nearby hospital and it changed her life.

"Who I am has changed in very meaningful ways since that experience." Robin realized how she had allowed herself, through busyness, to avoid deeper feelings and needs. "I know now I was in that place because I hadn't tried to strike a balance in my life. The best way I can describe it is my life was like a running track with a big hole in it, but I was busy enough that I just kept jumping over the hole as I ran around and around the track. But when things happened that couldn't be helped like my grandfather's death I wasn't running fast enough and I fell into the hole." She began to understand that her strong desire to do things alone and not ask for help also had isolated her. "I always wanted to do things by myself and that meant I didn't reach out to other people. Perhaps I had a confused notion of what being self-determined means. Self-determination now means taking care of myself and doing things I need to do *for me,* and therefore, I am determining my own mental health. That is my new self-determination."

The insights Robin gained have given new direction to her life. "Now instead of running around that track so quickly I am trying to walk so I can see the 'holes' coming up and I think that is part of the journey of self-awareness. You can't always predict when one of those holes is going to show up in your life—is it around a death? An illness? You can't always predict them, but if you know yourself well enough you can begin to recognize when you are losing yourself."

A year after her breakdown Robin sees her life as "very fulfilling." Her relationship with her husband has deepened, her young son brings her great joy, and her new work assignment is satisfying. Self-awareness and balance are key for her in maintaining stability and peace. "I force myself to think about things that I used to try not thinking about. I try to let myself feel things and not be cut off emotionally from situations that I had always avoided before in my efforts to be strong. I know now that allowing myself the emotional journey has been a very important part of my healing."

As a working mother of a young child she finds it challenging to maintain balance in her life. She recently started taking her son to day care for a short time before she goes to work. "Sometimes I go to the gym to work out and sometimes I just treat myself to a scone at my favorite restaurant. I just realized that five dollars and a little time to myself are well worth my mental health." Still, there are times Robin is thwarted by her desire to be liked. "My main obstacle is I don't want anybody to not like me." To stay connected to her self-determination and power Robin has discovered the word No! "The use of No! is the biggest way I claim power. No, I am not going to do that. No, I won't meet that request. No I can't do that right now, it's just too much for me."

As a result of her experience Robin has a mission to help other people deal with their depressions. "What happened to me was huge and I want other people to understand there is nothing that is worth your physical or mental health. I talk about my depression very openly and I can't believe the number of people who have responded. I have been really surprised about how my experience has helped me help other people."

She has no qualms talking about her experience and often in humorous terms. "I did a presentation to a group and I titled it, What I Did with My Summer Vacation. I asked the group, I went to a psychiatric unit...what did *you* do?" Her humor has helped her over the years. "It has always been a big part of who I am and how I deal with things. I now try carefully not to hide behind or just escape into humor as a way of avoiding real issues."

Robin has a deep desire to help others "take care of themselves and to know what they need for their care." She well understands how hard it is for women to pay attention to their needs. "You just always have to be so attentive to yourself because when you are overly attentive to everybody else you will lose yourself, literally. I have been using the metaphor of identify theft. When we just keep giving and giving of ourselves to other people without giving to ourselves it's much like giving out our social security number and credit card numbers. People will steal our identity and try to make us into what they want us be." For Robin, self-awareness is the key.

"If you know yourself well enough you can prevent any identity theft from happening."

Gretchen ✗ Eyes Wide Open

The past year has been a time of deep reflection for Gretchen as she sorts out what's next for her life. With the recent deaths of her sister, father, dear friend, and three young children from the school she runs, she's been propelled into sorting through decisions she's made over the years and where she goes from here. "I think I have some other things to do, and right now I'm wondering what they might be."

Throughout her life Gretchen has been a "questioner," seeking answers to the big questions about her life, and life in general, "I've always had huge questions about human destiny and what it means to be alive. What can I do? Those have always been big questions that seem to come from an almost unknown space." Recently new questions about her life path have come up and although she has not discovered all the answers, she is sure about wanting to "live life with my eyes wide open."

Gretchen does just that. She approaches situations by asking, *What is needed and am I going to do it?* She reconciles herself to the yes or no answer and then moves forward with creativity and energy. "I think I have never held life at arm's length. I believe I have experienced the sadness and losses in their fullest.

I think what I have found is a way to experience life and observe life almost simultaneously."

Time for reflection is essential for Gretchen. "In my life I make time to walk everyday in the early morning with my dog. I get up, put on whatever clothes it takes to be comfortable, and just walk. I do it because I need time to be reflective. My mental 'file drawers' are full and I just need some time to chew on things."

Her belief in the wonder of each person has led her to the decision to "lead a tiny, sort of backyard hobby into a place [a school] that really made a statement about a philosophy of not only education, but living." Initially, years ago, when Gretchen made the decision, that philosophy was not familiar to others where she lived. "Sometimes it was like speaking a foreign language. And not only did I get blank looks when talking about the philosophy, I also got a 'how dare you' response for bringing an alternative education to the community."

She was raised in a time when she was told in a "multitude of ways" that "good girls and good women make sure everybody is comfortable." By bringing a new educational philosophy to town she realized with surprise that some folks were feeling very uncomfortable. It was a turning point in Gretchen's life. "At first I wanted to stop what I was saying and try to make them comfortable. Then I came to understand that people change only when they are ready to change. We can't, and should not, force that upon one another. Really, our life is our own life to live the best we can. I realized that I would not intentionally hurt another individual even though sometimes I was making them uncomfortable. Those two were not the same things."

That awareness led her to examine her marriage and make new, painful decisions about not continuing the relationship, as well as understanding she could be a different role model for her daughters. "I can see some of this playing out in their young adult lives now, and making choices about their lives. They are generous, kind, understanding, and willing to say what they think." It also contributed to Gretchen's effectiveness as a leader, "We have hired young women right out of high school who haven't known what they wanted to do. I think when these young women watch me stand up and say, I think this is where we need to go right now, maybe somewhere in their life they go home and say, Well, it is right because I think it is right, and then they create the life they want."

Gretchen knows that no matter what comes her way she will approach it courageously, "I think when I am handed an unfamiliar challenge or circumstance I first say, I am going to get out of bed and do what I need to do, and then draw on everything I can muster to make wise decisions." Her greatest fear is whether she will have the energy and stamina to persevere. She understands, however, that "None of us really does anything alone. I think it is very important to feel humanly powerful. I think each of us *is* humanly powerful. The greatest sense of powerfulness, though, comes when a group of people act together and that can occur when people are engaged in community."

Gretchen has a unique perspective on the issue of courage and danger; two concepts that are often linked together. "I think maybe we should redefine danger. I think there is grave danger in squandering one's life; what a terrible loss that is—when people decide not to pursue some passion, to walk away from an opportunity or to not look at the day with open eyes. I think those are the biggest dangers. I think it takes courage to act on passion—to explore it, to turn it over, ponder it and determine its authenticity, and then act."

Sondra ✖ It's My Turn Now

When it comes to stepping up and taking on new, unexpected situations by redefining oneself, Sondra is an expert on the topic. All her life she has been willing to take on new roles, new jobs and new relationships, often in very short order. Much of the courage underlying her flexibility in redefining herself comes from her belief that there is not anything she could not do if she wanted to.

At sixty-eight, Sondra has a long life of courage to reflect on. The "most courageous" thing she ever did was when she was a sophomore in high school. She was asked out by the captain of the football team who tried to rape her on their date, and although he did not succeed, he told everybody he did. As a result, she was "ostracized" for several months by most students, and she had to make new friends and find new activities in which to be involved. In essence, she had to muster up the courage to find a new role for herself. Sondra discovered for the first time that she could successfully reinvent herself.

After college Sondra and her husband moved to a very isolated small town in northern Michigan so he could run his family's farm. It was the start of a very lonesome time for her. "I went from a life of being active and involved to just total solitude. But I did what I thought I was supposed to do; I think it was the *Ladies Home Journal* that came out with the togetherness thing that was supposed to be what marriages were about."

One night, though, sitting in the bathtub reading Betty Friedan's seminal book, *The Feminine Mystique,* she realized that there were other women who felt the same way she did. "In my whole life it was *the* defining moment for me." She began to talk with other women, join local organizations, and when she received an unexpected request to run for a county political position, she accepted. Her successful campaign and ensuing role on the County Commission started her on a lifetime of highly visible and influential positions. "All of a sudden I was in this position with power to make things happen. It was very exciting!" It also led to her divorce.

Several years later, when she was in her mid-forties, Sondra decided to apply to law school—again redefining herself. She went to law school in the evenings and during the day did fundraising for a State Senator that eventually led to a management position in the state senate. At that point, as she was finishing up law school she had the idea that rather than practicing law she could explore the possibilities of being a lobbyist in Washington, D.C. instead. When she passed the bar exam, she quit her job, packed her belongings, got in her car and took off for Washington D.C.... without a job. "I remember driving off to the Capitol with Diana Ross blasting 'It's My Turn Now' in the background."

In her new role Sondra traveled around the country fund-raising for the president and his political party. She found the job "very exciting... and very stressful," but it became increasingly more obvious that she did not agree with the stances of the political party she was raising money for. So, at age fifty-seven, after developing a long-distance relationship, she decided to move across the country to give it a chance, thinking, *I can get a job!* And find a job she did—a job that once again turned into an opportunity to redefine herself.

Sondra met a woman affiliated with the local university at a fundraising dinner, who asked her what she thought about women and philanthropy. Never having worked with women givers, Sondra did not have much of an opinion, though she was willing to educate herself on the topic. The university, through their fundraising efforts, had noticed that women did not give the same amounts as men did, and they commissioned Sondra and her new acquaintance to find out why. Their research resulted in a book called *Reinventing Fund Raising: Realizing the Potential of Women's Philanthropy* which has become the bible on women's philanthropy, and led to Women's Giving Circles throughout the country. "It set off a national movement," and today Sondra is credited in magazines and books as the pioneer in the field.

In reflecting on her courage to change and reinvent herself so often throughout her life, Sondra says, "I guess I have always believed that I could do anything I wanted to do. I do have good self-esteem, but I had periods in my life where that has been completely shattered, too. I guess I'm a strong person. I'm willing to speak out and accept the consequences. I think oftentimes women are hesitant to take a chance or take a risk—to change, to challenge themselves, to not get stuck in old definitions. I just can't think of any other way to be or anything else to have done with my life—I've loved the way my life has gone!"

Nicholeen x 180 Degree Turnaround

Nicholeen personifies self-determination, and always has. "My mother would say I was determined from birth. I was born two months early, determined to make it into this world on my own time, in my own way." She has lived a hard life, but out of that she has created strength, meaning, and a clear vision for her future. Nicholeen is deeply motivated to help people realize their dreams by tapping into their own courage and self-determination.

She grew up in a dysfunctional family, and as a teen, turned to drugs, alcohol, and self-mutilation to calm her fears. Several times she was institutionalized for many months and received intensive therapy, but she ended up living on the streets. Nicholeen got pregnant when she was twenty and continued to live a life of desperation. "There was a day where I was making $110 an hour as a stripper, but couldn't pay my rent because of my drug habit. Or, I had $60 for the month to buy groceries for me and my daughter." But even as she held a 45-caliber handgun to her head trying to commit suicide, something inside told her she had a reason for living. Later, as she detoxed from her long methamphetamine addiction and reached the lowest point of her life mentally, emotionally and physically, she started asking herself what she really wanted from her life. "If there was one moment in my life where something changed, it was then." She realized there was a light of hope and allowed herself to start dreaming about her future, "I started asking how do I move forward? I began dreaming and I said to myself, well, if you're going to dream you had better do it."

Now, at age thirty, because of her determination to achieve her dreams her life has completely turned around. She is married to a supportive loving man, has three, beautiful healthy daughters, just earned her associate's degree, was recognized by *USA Today* as one of twenty outstanding students nationwide, served as president of her community college's Student Government Association and the local chapter of Phi Theta Kappa (an international honor society), and is beginning work on a bachelor's degree in business management. "I am so grateful... being grateful, that's one of the strengths that keeps me going."

Nicholeen had to dig deep to find the self-determination and courage to move from seeing herself as a victim to a woman who is fully capable of reaching her goals. "I did play the victim role for many years. But I have had the courage not to be the victim any longer, and to instead, venture out into not-so-comfortable situations and challenge myself. I've had the courage to come to terms with the past and recognize, yes, those bad things and those good things have made me who I am today."

Once of her greatest challenges she still faces everyday is a voice inside her that tells her she is not capable. "It's like I have a demon on my shoulder, talking into my ear saying, *You are not good enough.* In earlier days that voice stopped her from even dreaming; now it gives her pause for just a moment, "In the beginning it was a constant battle. Anything I tried, I heard, *No way, you are not good enough.* But now I recognize that voice and choose not to listen."

Nicholeen lives for lists—lists of her dreams and goals, and lists of daily steps for making them a reality. She shares those dreams with others and asks for insights about how they achieved their dreams. "I'm always inquiring, how did you do that? What did you do to get there? I want to learn through their struggles or the steps they took." She surrounds herself with ambitious people, usually women she sees courageously facing life's challenges. "I think every woman shows courage. I think it takes courage just to survive when one could give up. Those I am around approach life's struggles in different ways, but they approach them. Sometimes successfully and sometimes not so successfully, but definitely determined and not turning away."

Nicholeen's dreams are fueled by a sense that she has a divine purpose in inspiring others' self-determination. "I want to ignite this courage in others and help them unlock their pain and hurt. I want to tell them to dream the impossible because the impossible is never impossible." She wants women to have the courage to just dream and do. "I yearn to share with others that I know, from my own life, that it takes courage to dream. I'd say to every woman: have the courage to dream and the courage to believe in your dream and to believe in yourself."

Lynda ✕ Lessons from Home Repair 101

"I came to realize I always had the power. I just did not use it."

Lynda is a vivacious, outspoken woman who understands and speaks eloquently about power. As with most women, she learned it the hard way through times of feeling powerless and then discovering the joys of feeling empowered. In a new job and a new marriage she now feels quite satisfied with where her life is headed, "Everything I have done before has prepared me for this moment."

Education gave Lynda a strong sense of empowerment. She was married, raising a family and working part-time when she decided to go to nursing school. It was difficult balancing it all. But the decision to return to school was made easier by the dream she had held for her life since she was a little girl, "I always had a vision of being highly educated. From the time I was a small child I had a goal that I would be a college graduate and more." She struggled with the impact her schooling took on the time she had with her children and yet, she knew she made the right choice in working on her degrees. "I always felt alive in the classroom. That is where I felt I belonged. I loved that it kept me fresh and energized!"

While she is grateful for her years in nursing, Lynda also learned lessons there about being powerless. At one point in her nursing career she took a job in administration working for a difficult supervisor. "I felt completely powerless. It was very frustrating and it impacted everything—my confidence, my effectiveness, and my personal relationships. I felt trapped by golden handcuffs in a miserable job. I was terribly unhappy and felt powerless to do anything about it." It was a difficult time, but when she finally left the position she took an important awareness with her. "I came to realize that I always had the power. To me, power means freedom. I will not relinquish the notion that I am always free to do what I want and move on."

A family crisis continued Lynda's lessons. When her first husband was diagnosed with cancer she struggled with the unfairness of his illness and the need for her to assume all the household responsibilities. "At first I felt it wasn't fair that I should have to do these things. And then I thought, *Who's going to do them?* I didn't ask for the situation, but once I got my head around the realization that things had to be done and there wasn't anyone else to do them, I never looked back. I did things that I didn't think I could ever do." Although she had never paid the bills, handled the taxes, or done many home repairs, Lynda began taking on her husband's care along with managing the finances and doing all the home maintenance. So, while she may not have chosen to do these tasks, Lynda found herself doing them and doing them well. "It was empowering, absolutely empowering. I thought, *If I can do this, I can do anything!* and it prepared me to make the next step. I just kept reaching out and doing something everyday that scared me."

Her discoveries about her own capabilities helped her through her husband's death, "I realized I could survive it and go on, and that was extremely powerful for me." Her sense of empowerment also helped ease some of the self-doubt that had, at times, challenged Lynda in moving forward. "I have often underestimated my abilities; I assume everyone is brighter and more talented or accomplished than I am." Awareness and discipline have made it easier for her to overcome the self-doubt. "I just have to keep an awareness of what's going on in my head. I see the self-doubt and tell myself that it is probably unfounded; everybody is struggling just like I am. I focus on the contribution to be made." She has learned to stay present rather than running away when she feels fear or self-doubt. "There are times when I just want to crawl in a shell or just hide. I want to just run away, but I have learned not to do that over time."

Lynda's deep faith and strong will allow her to continue staying present. She relies on daily readings to keep her focused and courageous. "I define courage as moving forward and doing something even though you are scared to death. My faith is strong and I am determined to keep doing things that frighten me like expressing myself when it is unpopular and by telling the truth. There have been times when I thought, *Should I keep my mouth shut and go along to avoid the pain or should I be absolutely truthful and say what needs to be said?* I've never shut up yet. That's where my personal power comes from."

Marilyn ✗ Trusting the Truth

Marilyn's life has unfolded—numerous times—in ways she might have never imagined.

As a youngster raised in the 1950s, while she always felt she was capable and competent, her dreams were based on the cultural norms of the day. "When I was growing up power was all about finding the right man. Power for females was all about manipulating male energy or male power to be used on their behalf."

She fulfilled that dream by marrying a physician, "a very good man, a nice man, but a man who didn't share much of an emotional life with me." By the time she was in her early thirties she had two young children and was "unhappy in my marriage. I was also unhappy being a full-time mother because I was a born leader and did not have any real outlet for my energies." She became very depressed. "In those days women married to doctors didn't work [outside the home]." However, Marilyn was always a writer in one way or another, and as a way of easing her depression she decided to take a writing course at the local college.

The first writing assignment she did was "very logical, very clear, and very well-written in terms of spelling, punctuation and all that." When she got it back from her instructor it had only one statement written on the top of the page, *Give me something of yourself!* She continued throughout the semester to write about any topic other than herself. "I could not do what he asked me to do, to give something of myself." Finally, as the course was wrapping up she decided to try and write an autobiographical piece.

On the day of the final class she realized it was her last chance to meet her instructor's challenge. She was determined to go to class so when the babysitter didn't show up to take care of her children Marilyn did something she had never done before. She spontaneously put the kids in the car, drove them to the hospital where her husband worked, and unannounced, left them in his care for the few hours she would be in class. "I don't know what gave me the courage to do that because I had never behaved like that before. I was totally a good girl and never nagged in selfish or inconsiderate ways. Still today, I do not know where that came from. I just knew that I absolutely had to make it to that class." In class she reluctantly read her writing, "I started crying. I had never before written or spoken the truth about myself."

Marilyn's courage to speak honestly about herself changed her life. "The uncanny thing is that when I left the room that day

I knew my marriage was over. In writing about myself and my life, I affirmed to myself I was worthy. I realized I did not need a doctor–husband to be worthy, and that I could do something with my life." The divorce took her two years, and while she at times questioned her instincts, she knew there was no other option. "I just knew I had moved to a place where being honest about myself had undermined my reason for being married. My marriage existed because I did not have the courage to live my own life. I was living through someone else and I did not have the confidence that I mattered on my own."

Life wasn't easy after her divorce. Although Marilyn was well educated, because of the economy she couldn't find a job. "It was a very risky thing that I did, leaving my marriage and not having a job." She was very depressed knowing "these two little children are depending on me," and at many points she was financially desperate. She ended up selling antiques and standing in unemployment lines to pay the mortgage.

In researching other ways of making a living she decided to explore ministry. She applied to and was accepted at a school on the west coast, which would require major decisions involving her children. By that time her boys were a bit older, their father had remarried and could give them a stable home. But the turmoil she felt in thinking about her sons going to live with him should she decide to attend the seminary was a huge dilemma. While trying to make the difficult decision to move she had what she describes as a mystical experience. "It's not something I do frequently, but it was strange and I still cannot explain it. I am not a mystic and I rarely have those kinds of experiences, but all I know is that it happened." Based on the experience she typed up the letter of acceptance to the school and from that moment her life unfolded in wonderful ways. "I made a deep commitment to having my life used for whatever good it could be used for, and that commitment underlies everything that has unfolded in my life since then."

For Marilyn, courage is reflected in her willingness to let her life move in unexpected ways. "I think courage is doing what you know is the right thing to do in spite of fear, opposition or any other deterrent. It is knowing that your values are so important and getting yourself to those values to the extent that it overcomes your reluctance." The decisions she has made in her life continue to be shaped through listening to her authentic voice. "If you see yourself as a conduit of spirit and that you are trying to be useful in the world, then you are the instrument. Trust your gut. Trust your inner self about what is right. Don't trust the logic of things; use your logical mind to check out what your intuition is telling you."

Marilyn stays true to her commitment and values through her spiritual discipline that includes Buddhist meditation and prayer. She also does a type of meditative weight-lifting routine that allows her to focus on her body and stay mindful. "Staying in tune to your body is important because you can get stuck in your head." Friends are also an essential part of her life and from time to time she finds her way back to therapy. "I have a very problematic family of origin and those demons are still with me so I need to go back into psychotherapy at times." What keeps me going, too, is my very favorite quote by Audre Lorde, 'When I dare to be powerful, to use my strength in the service of my vision, then it becomes less important whether or not I am afraid.'"

Carol ✗ Fulfilling Lingering Dreams

"The good thing about aging is that I've lost a lot of the fear that seemed so intimidating when I was younger. It's the realization that there's very little to be afraid of. What are they going to do...tell me no? At this age I've heard *no* so many times in my life that it doesn't mean much."

Carol doesn't really listen to other people saying no anymore and as a result, she is a 52-year-old journalism major at a large university, living 170 miles from home on her way to completing a life-long goal.

It's not that Carol has been sitting around since high school when an incompetent English teacher squelched her dreams of writing. Instead, she got on with her life and pursued a career in nursing, first in oncology and then in neo-natal intensive care. When she decided to relocate her family to a small town on the shores of Lake Michigan, her career options became limited. Since most college programs meant she'd have a 90-minute drive to class, she continued to work in the field of nursing while also training as a massage therapist.

Nursing was the career that supported her through her divorce and while she was raising her sons as a single mother.

Again, not her dream, but a practical alternative. "There were times during those years that I was pretty frustrated and a little depressed trying to be a good parent, work full time and do it all alone. I realized it was up to me to figure out how to work it out. If I was not feeling great during a certain period, I knew it was up to me to make it temporary. I recall once when I was particularly down and depressed, my fifteen-year-old son came and sat by me and handed me a tape. He said, Mom you need to listen to Gordon Lightfoot because he always makes you feel better."

And with that, Carol recalled that years before she had set three goals for herself : 1) to raise her children in a small town, 2) to see a whale in the ocean and 3) to meet Gordon Lightfoot, her favorite musician since childhood. She had accomplished two out of three. It was time for a bold move. Carol bought a ticket for the next Lightfoot concert near her and took the $50 she had set aside to pay the gas bill to buy her way backstage if needed. It was a lot of money for anyone, and as a single mother it seemed like a huge extravagance. But she was determined. And sure enough, Carol was able to scalp a backstage pass and meet the entire band, including Gordon. "It was like the highlight of my life, next to having children." So Carol was three for three on her goals, but she still had a dream that was lingering.

When her youngest son went off to college, she started

classes at the local community college. She began by taking all the courses she couldn't take in nursing school—photography, American literature, and journalism. Soon she was working on the school newspaper and applying to a university. "It really feels like I am completing something that I always told myself I would do. I realized that if I didn't do this it would bother me to the end of my life that I never completed my education." Now she spends her weeks among college co-eds and her weekends with her new husband, a musician, in a small town on the lake. She's not sure where her degree will take her, but that doesn't scare her. "Probably the biggest fear that I have is becoming stagnant. Whatever I do is to keep from becoming stagnant."

Patty O. x Following the Natural Path

As a young girl Patty would stand by the front door on Friday afternoons, bags packed, ready to join her brother and father on their weekend boating jaunts. She wasn't invited to go along, but she was determined not to be left behind.

Patty had discovered her first love, the outdoors, early on. Even though her mother and father were city people, she always yearned to be outside, "I just wanted open space." Growing up she was enthralled by the TV show, "Michigan Outdoors," earning her an early nickname of Mort Neff in honor of the show's well-known host and outdoorsman. Her favorite high school course was ecology, and for practice in her typing class she brought in *Michigan Outdoor* magazines and typed the articles. She found sustenance in nature. So choosing a career was easy...or so she thought.

In the early 1970s the environmental field was not always welcoming to women. "It was mostly men and everybody would tell me that I wasn't going to be successful or make any money from environmental work." Even her family wasn't entirely supportive of her career choice. "I was strongly encouraged to be a secretary, not an environmentalist." But, despite the lack of support, she was clear. She wanted to work to support the environment. "I just did it. I paid my way through school and chose to go away [to college] even though people said to stay home to save money."

Her mother played an important role in her life during those years by quietly supporting her choices. "As a young girl my mother wanted to be an architect, but her father wouldn't let her. He gave the money to her brother so he could go to college to be an architect. Because of her experience, when I would question everything you could see it in her eyes that she really felt the same way."

Questioning the status quo and following her own course was familiar for Patty. "Although I was raised Catholic and attended 12 years of Catholic school I was lucky to have been raised at a time when they were teaching love and peace." Her school offered a college-like format, allowing her to choose classes that helped her learn about other religions, people and environments. "The nuns were all protesting the Vietnam War and they took us to the inner city to work in the soup kitchens. They brought in Hari Krishna members, gays and lesbians, and many other people. They broadened my view of the world and taught me to question things."

She set a new course for her life when she decided to apply

for a job where she didn't know a single soul. Patty was working in the city, but knew she wanted to live in a more rural area—around Lake Michigan and in the woods. She heard about a position in a small town near the Lake, went for an interview and got the job immediately. A couple of days later she packed up all her things and moved to the new place where she was completely alone. "I had never been on my own before. A couple of women I started working with couldn't believe I moved to a new place all by myself. I realized that always before in my life I was trying hard to make everybody happy. Being alone in a new town helped me find my own self and like myself better." After dreaming for many years about being near Lake Michigan, she found peace in watching the sunsets over the water and walking on the beach.

Other personal and professional decisions followed, taking Patty to another state for a short time and back again to her beloved Lake Michigan. She was delighted to find a position working in natural resources for a Native American tribe. At first she found the job exciting; her ability to look at situations with a broad view and ask important questions allowed her to impact environmental policies and practices, and she enjoyed working in a culturally diverse organization. However, because she was one of only a few female natural resource professionals working in the Tribe, combined with the dynamics of fitting in as a non-native working in a tribal community, Patty's work was very stressful.

"There are times when you are trying to find out what to do with your life and to make a change and you are afraid." Working for the Tribe was one of those times. The stress began to wear her down, but still she stayed in her job. "I was too scared to change." The worry about whether she could find anything in the environmental field in a small town kept her stuck. It took almost two years, but she finally found the courage to leave. "With some encouragement from friends I finally got up the nerve to send out my resume. When I finally had my first interview for a new job, I screamed I DID IT! as I drove away."

Patty believes her success in life, like her success at finding a new position where she feels welcome, comfortable and excited, comes from her self-determination. "I feel it [my self determination] is like an energy inside me. I made some courageous moves because I was finally able, despite feeling nervous and scared, to find the energy and will to just go out and do what I wanted to do."

Christie ✗ Listening In

"I think courage is listening to the little voice inside of you that tells you what is right and what is wrong. The times in my life when I have gotten in trouble are the times when I hear the little voice and shut it out because of other pressures, other people's norms."

As the song says, the road that has brought Christie to her current place of possibilities was long and winding. Her journey to the fulfillment of her dream included many stops along the way—a rocky marriage, a move to a new state, the birth of a daughter that almost took her life, and financial risk. But all along the route she's listened to that quiet voice inside telling her when she was on the right track.

She remembers being aware of her inner voice even as a young girl. Christie split her time between her divorced parents. During the school year she lived with her father and on breaks and summer vacation she traveled to be with her mother. It was an adjustment for her, not just in parenting styles, but also in being thrust from one group of friends to another. She learned to feel secure within herself no matter where she was. She vividly recalls the day, when at age seven, her father put her on the bus with her five-year-old brother to travel several hours to her mother's home. "I remember being on that bus with all those adults, not really knowing the way and yet, feeling ecstatic. I was so thrilled. I knew that I was going to have a new adventure. I remember thinking that if some stranger tried to come up and sit next to me, I could handle it. I don't know how to explain it, but I felt I could make my own way—I could take care of myself."

That sense of self-reliance supported Christie in ending her first marriage. She had married her college sweetheart, supporting him as he was discovering what he was "meant to do." Eventually he decided he wanted to further his education, requiring a move across country, cashing out their retirement savings, and Christie working more than full-time. "It felt like drudgery. I would wake up every morning, really unhappy and resentful. I didn't like how I felt or who the person was that I was becoming." She stuck with it despite many "indicators" that her marriage wasn't going to work out; she had to accept that her high hopes in his new career choice were not going to be realized. Fortunately for Christie, she's never really been afraid of being alone, and never felt she needed a man to take care of her or even believed she needed to settle down. "I have never had the traditional idea that a man needs to take care of me. I have felt that even if I was on my own to my dying day that I could take care of myself and be happy."

Christie made a new life for herself and found she had created deeper levels of self-determination and courage. She showed courage leaving her first husband and later on it was even more courageous to get married again. Taking another chance on love required her to overcome a lot of fear. "To find the courage I had to listen to the voice inside of me that was saying, *You can do this. This is right. This is what you are supposed to be doing.*"

Trusting her inner voice was never more important than when she gave birth to her first child. Always a healthy person, Christie was thrust unexpectedly into a sudden and almost fatal medical situation when an auto-immune syndrome erupted during her daughter's delivery. Christie was in and out of consciousness for a week and remembers overhearing her doctors saying there was a 75% chance that she would die before the end of the night. She also remembers clearly thinking in response, "No, I don't think so. I *am* going to make it." Certainly the pictures of her new baby girl that were tacked up around her bed gave her strength, but her denial of what the physicians were saying also had great power. "I never believed what they said. I did not buy into the situation being hopeless and I just kept saying to myself, I can do this, I can do this. And I did." Even when she was told she would probably be disabled in some way once the worst was over, or at the very least, would need a liver or kidney transplant, she again refused to believe it. Despite their predictions she made a full recovery. "I believe in the power of the human will. My story is that I refused to believe what others were saying and found some power within me to help the doctors heal me. I made an active choice to live!"

Today, Christie lives in gratitude for her health, marriage, daughter, extended family, and her deep friendships with other women. She finds that her women friends keep her grounded and connected to herself, and inspire her to reach for more. Christie has noticed that the more honest they are with each other, the deeper and more precious the friendships become. "We're really authentic with each other now—we call each other on the carpet when needed and support each other unconditionally when that's needed."

And support is an important commodity right now as she begins fulfilling her dream of owning an art gallery. An artist herself, Christie has spent years envisioning a space that showcases her work as well as other artists. She is wildly excited about her new endeavor, but knows it is not without significant financial risk. She faces her fear by reflecting on what she learned about trusting herself during her earlier health crisis, "I really trust that this is the path I need to follow. There is no one saying that I have to stick to this path I have chosen. If it's not working I will find another path and see where that takes me." Christie taps into her courage by listening to the quiet voice inside. "I think in the purest form courage is just about listening to that voice inside you. I believe we were all born with it, no matter what your upbringing was. I try to always listen to it and be true to it."

Eva ✳ Rooted in Power

Like the tree that is a symbol for much of her life, Eva stands tall and strong. She's a mother, tribal leader, writer, storyteller and poet dedicated to being a healing force.

As a result of her many roles she has a deep understanding of power. Eva tells stories to illustrate her belief that the secret of life lives within our hearts, as does power. "Real power is collective power, it is the power of sharing a common dream. It is the power of sharing a common tree, and building a strong tree within a family and community. Collective power is a more complete kind of power—it is a healing power."

The tree metaphor winds its way through many of Eva's life stories and for good reason. She grew up in a family that was very poor and as a young person she was acutely aware of the differences that existed between her situation and those of her neighbors. "It sometimes created despair for me to feel like I wasn't as good as other people." As a Native American living in a non-native community she experienced a great deal of prejudice, and felt a sense of alienation from other people.

But she had a number of things going for her that helped ease her despair. Her mother and grandmother were very strong people and taught Eva early on that she had the capacity within herself to create her own destiny. "I had the benefit of a mother who could see very far. She and my grandmother took a larger view of life and had this amazing compassion for people." Because of her experience with these strong, hardworking women, Eva takes exception to the stereotype of Ottawa women being passive. "Somehow the stereotype is that we walk one step behind the man and are laid back, passive. The Ottawa women in my family were strong and influential!"

Eva was also a very good student; she did well in school and she found that empowering. She quickly learned that education represented a hope for her to achieve greater things and she worked hard at her studies. Now, as an adult, she sees education as a key to self-determination. "It's really important to somehow educate yourself, not necessarily formally through a degree, but from the universe. It is a great blessing to find a vocation that is close to your heart, something you feel passionate about."

She spent a great deal of time as a child outdoors in the fields behind her home, playing in the grass and trees. "I was wealthy in the outdoors; I had everything I needed. I was liberated in the fields." There was also a huge elm tree, well over 100 years old, that provided her with comfort and perspective. Parts of the tree were decayed, but the roots fanned out in all directions, and were strong and firm. Then, as now, she saw that the tree "was very much like my life. Here is this really strong tree that has lasted for hundreds of years, an elegant tree, and yet part of it was decayed because of circumstances, like the circumstances over the generations within my family and Tribe. Somehow the ability to find spiritual inspiration has allowed me to reconstruct a strong tree in my family and to find a place of healing for myself."

The vision and metaphor of that tree has guided Eva through family and career decisions. In her work in the field of substance abuse she has helped other Native American people to heal. "This work is all part of a larger dream that I have for healing the big hole in the tree. This is part of me, my vocation, that has been close to my heart."

In her quest for healing she has often been in positions where courageously speaking from her heart has been needed. "That is part of the role of leadership to sometimes say a bold thing. I can tell you it isn't easy." She is learning to temper her voice sometimes, out of a deeper understanding of the difference between power and control. "Just because I feel a sense of my personal power doesn't mean that I have to control the situation through my words or actions. Each of us needs to find our own voice and I know there are effective ways of using mine."

Eva's contribution to her family and community is strengthened by the lessons she continues to learn about letting go. "Some of the hardest lessons I've learned have been around letting go. Wanting things to go in a particular way or setting out and seeing a particular vision on how life, my life, the life of my family or the life of my community should unfold, and then having to take a different course. Then wondering, *Is my dream not worth it? Is my dream incorrect? Am I way off base? Am I just a misfit?* There is serenity in learning when to just let go. And not only to let go and be bitter about it, but to really let go and see what happens. The wonder of letting go is often better than getting your own way."

It's Yours ✕ Own It

It's Yours ✗ Own It

I will not die an unlived life. I will not live in fear of falling or catching fire.
I choose to inhabit my days, to allow my living to open me, to make me less
afraid, more accessible, to loosen my heart until it becomes a wing, a torch,
a promise.

—D. MARKOVA

IF YOU WANT to clear a room of women, just suggest that you want to discuss the concept of power. As if by magic, everyone will suddenly recall a previous commitment to have a bikini wax, undergo periodontal surgery, or some other painful experience. Most women would do anything to avoid getting intimate with the topic of power.

The electricity that surrounds the word and throws most women out of balance comes from our direct connection with distortions of the concept. By the simple virtue of being female most of us have come face-to-face, whether in our families, our workplace, or even our religious institutions, with the attitude that power is the birthright of the other gender. And most women have found a way to survive, even master, living in the place of "under" in the power dynamic.

Glance at the bookstore shelves and you'll see how frustrated and confused women have become about power. Titles such as: *Nice Girls Don't Get the Corner Office; Hardball for Women: Play Like a Man, Win Like a Woman; The Princessa: Machiavelli for Women,* indicate that we see power as something women gain by emulating men's behaviors and then playing the power game to beat them on their own court.

Merriam-Webster's synonyms for power include: authority, jurisdiction, control, command, sway, dominion—meaning the right to govern, rule or determine. Power is defined as "possession of ability to wield force, permits authority or substantial influence." It's no wonder women are unwilling to own power in their lives!

THE OLD CODE

As women, we are so uncomfortable with power—ours and theirs (whoever they might be)—that we remain passive to avoid confrontation, hint instead of asking directly for what we need, and even withhold attention and affection to make an indirect point. We communicate in code and hope others will pick up on our needs and wants. By not expressing power, women do not fully express themselves.

Many of the women we interviewed are consciously aware

of times in their lives when they were perfectly happy to not express their power and stay in the people-pleasing mode. Happy for a short time, that is. When we asked them to cite examples of when they had exhibited power, they were quick to draw the distinction between the way the world defines power and the way they personally viewed it and used it. Over and over we heard from women that they are not comfortable with the word power or its currently accepted meaning.

Living and perpetuating the myth that there are two kinds of power has an enormous cost, not just for women, but for all of humanity. Allowing others to wield their determination over ours means that we give up our dreams in the fulfillment of theirs. Many of the women we interviewed described what it was like to lose themselves by getting caught up in the power of others' expectations. The cost of accepting and living in the current definition of power is too great. It can and does literally cost us our lives.

In our culturally accepted definition and current usage, we refer to the word power as a noun—we view it as a thing. We see it as something separate from ourselves, as in, "I *have* power. They don't *have* power. I used my power to get my way." Power, as noun, then becomes something sought, something avoided, something won or lost, something feared or coveted. Viewed as a noun, we believe power comes from a role, a position, an attitude, a birthright, or even a lifestyle. We often connect it in a causal relationship with money, assuming an increase in one assures an increase in the other. And, most destructively, we believe someone has to lose it for others to have it. As a noun, we ascribe finite properties to power as in *There is only so much power to go around—so I'd better get me some.* As a noun, we can't help but look at power as divisive.

And yet the word power has its root in the Old French word "poeir," meaning simply "to be able." It's a shame this uplifting word has developed the emotionally charged connotation of force, command, and rule. It's time for a new view of the word and it's true meaning to be revived—it's time for a new Code.

Why should we care if power is redefined? Why should we be interested in catalyzing a shift in the understanding of this concept?

Simply because the current approach is not working. It's ineffectual at best and downright oppressive at worst. Our current Code separates the world into power "haves" and "have-nots." It perpetuates the myth that we may, at any moment, find ourselves on the wrong side of the equation. We run ourselves into the ground trying to accomplish and accumulate all that we can to make sure power stays on our side. And our physical, mental, emotional, and spiritual bodies all pay the price. In several cases, women we interviewed described a breakdown as a result of this push to achieve. Fortunately, in all cases, it led them to re-evaluate their lives and shift to a healthier power image.

The common view of power that fosters competition and creates winners and losers limits our ability and even the capacity to collaborate. We believe we will be fulfilled and protected when we become the accepted group that has the right answers and, therefore, the power. And then we become disillusioned when we realize this limited view of power is erroneous.

We measure power by what's in our bank accounts, in our driveways, the accomplishments of our children, and the status of the organizations we belong to. We link power with success to justify our separation attitude and drive to accumulate. We use it to rationalize action over reflection and doing over being. Over time, women have grown (or, more appropriately, shrunk) to see the only Code for power as "over" or "under."

WOMEN'S RELATIONSHIP WITH POWER

Traditionally, women and men have had different relationships with power. We view it and react to it in differing ways. In *Closing the Leadership Gap,* Marie Wilson describes how, even at an early age, boys and girls behave differently in relation to power. She states, "When boys are mean, they are expressing their power and when girls are mean they are expressing their lack of power."

Our culturally accepted messages tell us that power comes to women and men at different points in their lives. As many sociologists have described, women possess traditional power relative to their ability to procreate. This starts when they are young, able to attract attention, and wield considerable sexual power over men, young and old. Women who don't grow beyond this definition may continue to use sex as a method of power and control in relationships. As a women passes through her child-bearing years, this so-called traditional power peaks and then diminishes with menopause. Ask any middle-aged woman about this phenomenon and she's likely to tell you exactly when she first felt the sting of age that made her invisible and powerless. As one fifty-something woman described it, "I was walking down the sidewalk one lunch hour feeling particularly confident and together. After passing several men I realized that they all seemed to be looking past me, like I wasn't even there."

Conversely, male power has been traditionally linked to the creation of wealth and status afforded by their profession. Since younger men have less earning potential, they are seen as having less power and often exhibit more anger because of it. As men age and their income grows, they become attractive to a wider group of potential partners. Even older men are described with words like virile or potent, which correspond to their higher income level and therefore, their perceived power. Men who don't move beyond this definition of power may continue to view sex as their right—they've earned it.

For men, traditional power increases with age; for women, it decreases. This explains why so many women feel a surge of personal power (connection with their authentic self) when they reach menopause as they no longer fit the youth-related definition of power. At midlife we arrive at a place of unwillingness to simply accept the boxes and boundaries of our lives. We begin to define power in our own way, in our own style.

At any age women's relationship with power has the obvious slant of "power-under." You only need to look as far as the political leadership of even the most developed nations to see that women are not yet filling the key power roles.

Religion oftentimes reinforces the patriarchy and the male model of power. We're brought up on images of God as Father or his Holy Son. When Sue Monk Kidd wrote about her awakening to the Divine Feminine in *Dance of the Dissident Daughter,* she described what it was like to "collide with the patriarchy" within her church, her faith tradition, her marriage, and also within herself. She introduces her book by saying, "The female soul is no small thing. Neither is a woman's right to define the sacred from a women's perspective."

Within the big three power arenas in our culture—money, politics, and religion—it's easy to see why women have had a hard time linking their name with the word power. Unless, of course, it's to say something like, *My power is less than....* We still are seeing relatively few examples of power in our images and messages. Our devalued role in society still haunts us.

In *The Shadow King: The Invisible Force That Holds Women Back,* Sidra Stone describes her understanding of this collective struggle with power. She writes,

> As I came to know my own Inner Patriarch and those of other women, a clear pattern emerged. I could see how our Patriarchs keep us in an inferior position—if not in our work, then in our relationships. They make us distrust ourselves. Even more important was the discovery that they make us distrust other women as well...I saw again and again how the Inner Patriarch devalues us and what we did just because we were women.

Women disassociate from the word power because of its close link with force, control and brute strength. We would rather go around an issue or problem than use fist banging to find a solution. The way power is currently defined is not our style.

Trouble is, many of us haven't found our style and so we don't connect with our power. We just go along. In doing so, we slip back into power-under. We need to redefine power in its broadest sense, so we see other options beyond expressing power as violence or dominance.

If we want to know how we think about power, we need to look at the women in our lives. "We think back through our mothers and grandmothers if we are women," says author Virginia Woolf. If we agree that women today are uncomfortable with the notion of power, then it is because we are our mothers' daughters. We are our history. For most of us who are in our middle years that means we saw our mother's generation get literally and figuratively swatted around by power.

During World War II, our mothers were called into the workforce to supplement the male labor shortage and shore up the war efforts. From 1940 to 1945 the number of female workers rose by 50 percent. Women became streetcar conductors, taxicab drivers, business managers, commercial airline checkers, aerodynamic engineers, and railroad workers. Women operated machinery, drove ambulances, buses, cranes, and tractors. They unloaded freight, built dirigibles and gliders, worked in lumber mills and steel mills. In essence, women occupied almost every aspect of industry. Women were even responsible for carrying on the tradition of the great American pastime—baseball.

When the men came home women were systematically shut out and turned away from the workplace and the baseball diamonds. Although the media did its best to extol the virtues of being the master of one's own kitchen, women lived with an underlying angst and anger regarding the power dynamic that told them to go home and stay there. But for the most part they did.

Women created picture-perfect homes and raised well-behaved children. Their power came from their ability to do such tasks with grace and seeming ease. They supported their husband's career because it paid off in their power structure as well. The roles were well-defined, the rules were rigid. Women often gave their power away in the trade-off of being taken care of. Even if a woman wanted to enter the workforce there were few opportunities, especially if she was married. (One of the women we interviewed had to start lying on her job applications because companies wouldn't hire a married woman!) And many husbands of that era refused to entertain the notion of their wives working because it posed a threat to their own power status. The popular refrain, "No wife of mine is going to work," was based on the fear that the husband's power among his peers would be diminished if it were perceived that he could not support his family without the help of a woman.

Fortunately, while our mothers were raising their daughters, they sent another message. Some whispered it to us, some openly drilled it into us, some feverishly pushed us, but the message was clear—"Do as I say, not as I do! You can be and do anything you want." So we were raised by women who encouraged us to live out our dreams—and we did! Many of the women we interviewed credited their mothers with flaming their desires and holding the door open for them to run through toward meaningful lives.

In the second women's movement in the 1970s women entered the workplace *en masse*. We bought the expectation that traditional power would make us happy. We stepped into the power structure with very few of the skills needed to navigate the system. The women who went the farthest were those who walked, talked, and dressed the part. Who can forget those Dress for Success days when a man, John Malloy, told us how to look the part of power? In blue suits and pink rosette ties, we became just smaller men. We thought we wanted what they had, and that by adopting their definition of power we would find happiness. Instead, this left no time for our families, our friendships, or ourselves. We saw our choices as mutually exclusive—career or family.

By still defining power as position, status and money, we were just giving ourselves options as to who would make it—him or me. We fought with our sisters as we competed for power jobs in organizations and bullied those who chose to stay at home into thinking they were less than us.

The next wave of working women saw the trap of the power struggle and decided to take another approach. They became the poster women for "I can do it all!" No choosing necessary—they believed it was simply a matter of time management and multitasking and every woman could have a high-charged career with a well-adjusted family posing on the cover of *Home Beautiful*. And so we lived, and we use the term very loosely, in an era when we were led to believe that being Superwoman was the real way to power and ultimately, happiness. As the connection with our souls grew dimmer (who had time for yoga or journaling or even a hot bath?) the prescriptions for Prozac rose. The media was beating it into our heads that now we should be happy and fulfilled, and instead we were just plain full.

Fortunately, our daughters were getting the message even if we weren't. They were playing on soccer teams and not taking winning and losing like it was life or death. They were forging different relationships with boys as peers instead of potential protectors or future income sources, and not going underground with their opinions and intellect. They were participating in programs that helped them learn to say no and learn how to lead. They continue today to develop skills and gather tools to shift the power paradigm and it's our responsibility to not just cheer them on, but to work side-by-side to solidify this change.

AVOIDING POWER

We don't consciously set out to avoid our powerful nature. Rarely do you hear a woman declare that she woke up with a renewed sense of how important it is for her to be disconnected, frantic, and fearful. Yet, everyday we foster thoughts that drive our behaviors and actions that allow us to avoid connecting with ourselves and our power. These thoughts and behaviors are as diverse as the population of women; however, they do cluster into three predictable patterns.

1. Avoiding by Keeping Score

The first pattern of thoughts and behaviors that keeps us from embracing our powerful nature is that of keeping score. When we operate from this place we look for ways to compare ourselves to others. We constantly look to see how we measure up and focus on how we are perceived.

We say things to ourselves like, *With all my credentials, I'll beat out all the other candidates,* or, *I don't have what it takes to go back to school; everyone else is younger and smarter.*

We see situations and interactions as competitions and try to get "a leg up" on the other person in order to get ahead. Or we blame our lack of happiness on others and the situations we think they have created: *I'd be happy if only they would see I deserve the promotion,* or, *If only he'd get a better paying job, then we could live a better life.*

From this place of keeping score or comparison, we think and believe that we are not enough—we are not worthy. We find ways to compare ourselves to others to simultaneously prove we're better than some and not as great as others. It's a thought process that keeps us stuck in mediocrity as we find comfort in being somewhere in the middle.

It allows us to avoid power by not taking chances or risking a change that would prove we are worthy and unique. When we don't live up to our potential we shift the blame to others, see ourselves as victims, and become defensive. It puts a chokehold on our power by allowing us to play the safe role of victim as we wait for others to make the changes we ourselves need to catalyze.

When we operate from a keeping score mentality, we frequently feel put upon, frustrated at our lack of options and mired in self pity. Because our behavior follows our thoughts, we unconsciously create drama in our lives that reinforces being in power under. We miss a deadline for financial aid and have no choice but to delay going back to school. We take on more responsibility at work than we can handle and when we fail, we blame the system and lack of support. We stay in unsatisfying relationships waiting for the other person to change and denying that we have any work to do ourselves.

While not operating out of this competitive ring of thinking all the time, chances are when we're stressed or tired or feel threatened we unconsciously respond from a place of keeping score. A tough budget meeting at work can easily show up as *How come I'm the only one who has to cut expenses?!* When we're in this place we're disconnected from our power through the projection of the situation as seen outside of us. We can't and don't want to see how we play a part in creating the drama—how we want to make our own self-worth issues someone else's problem. From this place we don't accept our power because it's easier to thrust it upon others and blame them when we realize we have none.

2. Avoiding by Keeping Peace

The second set of behaviors and thoughts is more evolved in its approach. Here we see that we have a hand in what we create, but unfortunately feel responsible for everyone and everything else as well. We operate from a place of wanting to keep the peace at all costs. To avoid any possibility of conflict or confrontation that might ruffle feathers or stir the pot we go along with what others think and want so they will view us as cooperative, great team players, and supportive friends or spouses. We keep our needs and our power under wraps and focus instead on making sure others' needs are taken care of. The trouble with this approach is, as one wise woman put it, "If it's peace at any cost, then the cost of peace keeps going up."

Our self worth issues play out in the form of believing everyone else's needs are more important. As women, we've had a lot of practice and plenty of role models for this approach. We've been socialized to believe that this is our role as wife and mother and even as executive assistant and church deacon. In our society the supportive role is seen as having a glory of its own.

In our quest to keep the peace, we try to anticipate everyone's needs and fulfill them in an unspoken exchange for getting our needs met. The unconscious deception is that we expect others to meet our unexpressed needs and then do a slow boil when they don't. These thoughts keep us enabling addictive behavior and feeling good about our role as martyr. We avoid our true power by feeling *false* power in propping someone else up (and in the meantime, keeping them from embracing their own power). Statements that begin with *I need, I want, I am* are foreign to us because we're focusing on creating harmony that we perceive comes from doing and being what we think others want.

As with keeping score, we might not hang out in this place the majority of the time, but in every instance where we go along with the crowd when we have another idea, opinion, or desire is a moment when we've stepped into this cycle and out of our power. At that moment, we've made a decision to disconnect from our true north and stay unconscious.

3. Avoiding by Keeping Strong

When we evolve to a place of understanding that the expression of our needs and wants is actually a good thing, we usually spend some time hanging out in a pattern of thoughts and behaviors that keeps us strong and competent. The good news is we're starting to see that we matter; the bad news is we believe we have to prove that we do. We show the world the tough exterior of fierce independence and the utmost in competency. We reinvent everything to put our stamp on it and look at collaboration as an unnecessary slow down in the process. We are impatient, perfectionistic, and think the world would be a better place if everyone would just do it our way.

This approach is very much rewarded and even revered particularly in American business today where women are told by such icons as founder and editor of Currency/Doubleday, Harriet Rubin, to "become hyperaggresive and hyperdetermined because business is about intense daring and a reckless abandon to succeed." Unfortunately, there is no room in this approach to make a mistake or even admit you might not know.

When we operate with thoughts of keeping strong, we dismiss alternative approaches and don't allow others to learn at their own pace. We feel powerful because we feel like we're in control which is actually a masking of our self-worth problems with "power over" everything and everyone one. It's not a place where we are comfortable with statements like "I don't know" or "What do you think?" The irony of this thinking pattern is that it is actually encouraged and rewarded in our current power paradigm. It's the basis for the "lone cowboy"—the American dream where someone trumps his way to the top and is allowed to simply run over others.

As women, we're less inclined to adopt this strategy as our way of avoiding authentic power. But if we do, we're labeled "bitch" or "user" while our male counterparts are applauded. But we do find times when our drive to prove ourselves has us discounting and devaluating others and acting before evaluating the impact on the whole. We know we have flipped into keeping strong and competent when we find ourselves flying solo and doing it all on our own.

A NEW CODE

In truth, power, as its root hint, is an adjective—a word used to describe or identify. Power means *I am able, you are able, we are able.* As we expand our understanding of the word we expand our interaction with the concept. Some of the women we talked to have begun to see power as a part of themselves, something internal, something already integral to their being, not something they must obtain. They have begun to live by their own Code. They are owning the fact that they *are* power.

These women are living the truth that power lies in each individual and that it is our responsibility to cultivate it within ourselves and each other.

There's an important distinction to be made here. Many books, tapes, and workshops talk about people owning their power, again presenting power as a thing they have accumulated. If we own our power we're simply laying claim to something again outside of ourselves. It also suggests that at some point, we'll lose it.

The new Code calls us to see *we are all able, we are all power.* By virtue of being human, we each *are* power. There is no more/less or over/under, but simply the knowledge that each and every individual is an equal source of power. Although there may be unique expressions and gifts that express power in individualistic ways, we are all sources. The new Code calls us to own it—*we are power.*

SEEING NEW POSSIBILITIES

So what would a new Code include? What would it look like and who would connect with it? Most importantly, how would it change the world?

In September 2004, Eve Ensler, during her opening address to 1,200 women gathered at Omega Institute's Women & Power Conference, shared a vision for a world with greater balance, a world that honors women's compassion and wisdom. The profound creator of *The Vagina Monologues* and V-Day, spoke about a new way of looking at power defined by words such as "include, inspire, lift up, be with, let go, sharing, expanding, power in service of, seeking solutions not revenge, collaborating, inviting." Eve believes that women will be the "carriers of the new paradigm."

A new Code would look like the women in this book. The women you are meeting here have opened themselves to embrace a richer, fuller and deeply truthful definition of power. It hasn't always been easy, or even fun, but the words they use to describe this place of power that they are now living include: exploding, amazing, interesting and full of challenge, meaningful, and intriguing. Who wouldn't want that?

Through their experiences we can see that three significant shifts begin to take place in ourselves and in our world when we open to a new definition of power:

1. We shift from little "s" to big "S."

The first significant shift that occurs naturally when we see power as an adjective is we move from the small "s" of self, defined from our ego, to our capitalized "S" Self, defined by our connection with our authentic Self, our true Self, our Soul.

Our ego-self looks to power as something we either have to get or something we will never have. It is our ego-self that will use any means available to compare ourselves to others in an effort to elevate or destroy our feelings of self worth. It is our ego that has us constantly looking outward to see how we measure up in our job, in our relationship, in our physical appearance. And the ego is more than happy to point out where we're falling behind. It is our ego that wants to place us under or over others. Our ego keeps us from acknowledging and coming to peace with all parts of ourselves and loving what is.

As Rachel Naomi Remen, M.D., and author of the books *Kitchen Table Wisdom* and *My Grandfather's Blessings* writes:

> Often healing is not becoming more than who we are, it's undoing the way we have fixed ourselves in order to win the approval of those around us. It's returning to our own integrity, even though the integrity may, at first, feel unfamiliar because we've never lived from there before. It's reclaiming the parts we've put in our shadow. And some of those parts may be very powerful and positive parts for which we could not get acceptance from the people around us. So it's more like an uncovering process, rather than an adding on of something new.

It is our deep healing that takes us into our capital "S" Self—

our connection with Source, Creator, Goddess or whatever term you use—that knows we are here to remember we are already perfect and whole and do not need fixing or completing. As an individual spends more and more time experiencing life and expressing herself from this place of deep connection to Self, her sense of power increases significantly.

From this place of connection with Self, we begin to see and treat ourselves differently. We see our value. Our gifts and our unique perceptions as women, those of compassion, inclusion, and service to others start to take on real value regardless of what the rest of the world says. We begin to care for ourselves and we take care. We nurture these feminine traits and stop pushing ourselves to be something we're not—namely men—in order to fit into the world's definition of power. It's from this place of respect and acceptance of ourselves that we can truly respect and accept others. We can visualize a changing world not because "they screwed it up and now we're going to fix it," but because we all have a stake in changing the world together.

Many women we interviewed drew the distinction between the old Code and the new Code they are now connecting with. They are attempting to find language that expresses the feelings and sensations associated with experiences of authentic power. Feelings of lightness and rightness and clarity. This new language separates power from previous external experiences that felt oppressive, dishonoring, and even unnatural.

2. We understand it's less about action.

The second shift that occurs when we embrace the true nature of power is understanding that reflection and contemplation are equally as important as action. We shift our intention from action, as a means of proving or getting more power, to action with a connection to our inner wisdom.

From the mis-definition of power as a noun, we are catapulted into a world of do, do, do in the struggle to get power. Endless goals, to-do lists and over-focus on personal accomplishments are the outcroppings of our organizations and companies that live by the mantra grow, grow, grow—regardless of the cost.

When we are no longer driven to accumulate and accomplish in order to prove our worth, we can see the value in reflecting and stopping to check in with our inner compass, our true north, to make decisions that support our internal growth and evolution. This compass that resides in each of us is only accessible when we take a break from the never-ending lists and voices of others who compel us to live in Shouldville and Have-To-Haven.

Almost without exception, the women we talked to identified specific ways in which they took time to stop and simply listen for what was truly important to them. Some used prayer or meditation, others journal, and still others use exercise and a connection with nature. Regardless of the method, they told us that without their process they find themselves caught up in the whirlwind of societal expectations and endless to-do lists.

It is critical to understand that refocusing from action to reflection does not mean that we never do or accomplish, but rather we value both and experience both. As Thich Nhat Hanh says, "Meditation is not to escape from society, but to come back to ourselves and see what is going on. Once there is seeing, there must be acting. With mindfulness, we know what to do and what not to do to help."

Action without reflection keeps us questing for power outside ourselves in the next thing we purchase, the next degree we earn, the next job we land. Because we give more credence to those things outside ourselves, we listen more closely to the voices outside us as well. We perceive our power as under their level of power.

For example, we may follow the advice of others who tell us that completing a M.B.A. will provide the ticket to a higher paying job and happier existence even though our heart may be telling us to complete shiatsu training and open our own clinic.

By ignoring our heart and following others we negate our power and give more value to theirs. An expanded, truer definition of power requires us to reflect and respond from our heart, instead of reacting to others' ideals.

Reflection also means that we consider the impact of action on the whole system involved. We see the whole picture and take all the nuances into consideration. We ask, how will this impact other aspects of my life? How will this affect other people? What is the cost to the larger world?

Several of the women we interviewed wrestled with decisions that would uproot their lives—to go back to school or to change careers. They stated it was essential to reflect on what impact it would have in order to discuss, negotiate and prepare for those changes from a place of respect for all. It would be easy in this situation to flip into power-over and just declare your needs and what you intend to do about it, as in "I'm going back to school and I know it will cause scheduling difficulties, but I don't care—I have to do this." Or to slide back under by thinking other's needs are more critical with a statement such as: "I'd like to change jobs, *but* I know it will disrupt our lives so I won't do it."

Taking the time to go inward and giving others time to reflect on their needs moves us from "but" to "and"—taking into account and respecting the needs of all. It would look like: "It's important for me to complete this degree. I know it will shake things up *and* I'm interested in how we can manage these changes together." As women we are more likely to put others' needs ahead of our own—seeing more power in others at the exclusion of ours. Reflection keeps us honest with ourselves by connecting with and valuing our needs equally.

3. We make the move from competition to collaboration.
When we understand that at the core everyone *is* power and that it is not based on works, roles or achievements, then we begin to experience the true value of collaboration. This new experience allows us to work and connect with others from a place of mutual respect and care that strengthens us both. In essence, when we can move beyond the illusion that you have to lose so I can win, we are able to create opportunities for us to both win. In a relationship, it means: *I express my needs fully and listen respectfully to yours as well.* It doesn't mean: *I listen so I can develop a case to convince you that my needs are more important or my solution is better.*

Collaboration means we listen with an ear towards understanding and looking for solutions. It does not mean just "getting along" or "going along." Liz Dolan, then Global Marketing

Director for Nike, recounts a pivotal moment in her work life when collaboration, not just keeping the peace, was instrumental in claiming her power.

Once I had a difference of opinion about the strategy for a particular project with the employee who headed that project. And at the end of our tenth conversation, he finally said, Well, Liz, I guess you and I just disagree. That was the moment of truth for me as his boss because I thought, Okay, we just disagree. Does that mean I fold? Or do I just say my vote counts more than yours? Ultimately, I did say, You're right, we disagree, and so here's the way we're going to do it. It was one of the hardest things that I ever did. As women, we are raised to be the peacemakers. Our instinct is to find common ground. Sometimes it just doesn't work. And those are ugly moments.

When we can come from this place of open, honest and direct communication we can create workable solutions. Because it is collective, the solution is always greater than the single solution of one. This significant shift means that we adopt a respect for all—all people, all creatures, all of nature. We see nothing and no one as having more power, so we care for others as we care for ourselves.

For most of our lives, women have struggled with the ongoing dance of power. We've been taught by our experiences that money = power and power = control therefore, money = control. This toxic equation has kept many of us in disrespectful relationships and jobs believing someone else's money gave them power and control over our lives. It's that other Golden Rule that says: Those who have the gold, rule.

A new Code based on collaboration also means that resources such as time and money are seen as tools to share in the pursuit of problem solving and right action instead of possessions to be hoarded for annunciation of worth. For example, rather than keeping the profits, Eve Ensler signed over the rights to her hugely successful play, *The Vagina Monologues,* so local volunteers across the globe can raise awareness and funds to stop violence against women in their own communities.

This new understanding of power, *we are power,* frees us up from the bondage of believing that those with the most resources, money, time, or energy have more control or more say in how problems get addressed. If one individual brings more money to the solution (or relationship) and one brings more time, both can be seen as equal because both are forms of "being able."

We need to acknowledge that there is real economic value to the woman who chooses to stay at home and raise children or run the household so her partner can function exclusively in the realm of their career. Unfortunately, until we shift our definition, women who choose these roles are placed in power under in their relationships and in society. Even if a career woman opts-out for a few years it can have a tremendous financial impact. That places an incredible strain on the concept of equal power in a relationship unless both parties understand the true nature of the word.

The answer does not simply lie in an increase in women's pay. High earning, high-powered wives are no longer the enigma they once were. However, in relationships collaboration and communication are still necessary to juggle what we perceive as a power struggle based on resources.

Understanding each person is of equal power stature is the first step in learning a new dance. In fact, it's the only way to move out of dependence or looking for power through someone else. We step into the world of independence when we understand we are responsible for our own power and move towards the goal of achieving interdependence where we are comfortable sharing equal power with another.

CHOOSING POWER

It is important to understand that power is first and foremost a choice. We can choose to live from a place of unconscious reaction based on old patterns or we can choose to open to our healing and growth by consciously responding to our highest Self. That's not to say we just magically choose and then everything is better. Rather, we start with the choice to allow, affirm and embrace power, and embody it fully, and then true power begins to flow. At first it winds its way uphill over our personal and societal patterns, then gathers momentum as we have experiences that reinforce the world will not crumble into pieces if we respond from our power.

What can we expect when we live from the Code of authentic power? There are four hallmarks of owning it that rise to the surface:

1. Power is neutral.

The most startling change and perhaps most significant in its affect is that the connection with authentic power takes us to a place of being neutral about power. When we fully realize that *we are all power,* we drop the emotional charge we had in response to the concept. When we make the choice to see everyone as having authentic power, including ourselves, we are no longer bound by our reactions of power-under to someone else's power-over. It's not that this dynamic never happens again in our lives, but it becomes quite obvious when it does. From this place of connectedness and consciousness we can be aware and can choose to respond authentically.

2. Conscious choice creates power.

Just as it was with self-determination, an important hallmark of connection with this redefined power is understanding *every-thing is a choice.* When we live consciously and make choices from our higher Self connections, a shift happens. We begin to see the outward manifestation of our call for peace and happiness. We notice that our lives function with a new level of ease because, as author Byron Katie says, we view "everything as happening for us, not to us." Living consciously means we acknowledge that we create our life—every bit of it. So we begin to choose more wise-ly. When we live unconsciously—shit happens—drama, chaos, and turmoil are a regular part of our existence because we invite them in by keeping our eyes closed to what is truly happening. So the options are shift or shit—we choose.

3. Power is everywhere in our lives.

Our new awareness highlights dimensions in our life where we are all connected as power. We may feel authentically powerful in our relationship with others, but regularly bury our head in the sand when it comes to our financial responsibilities. Or maybe we're fully engaged in meaningful work, but are doing little to express ourselves creatively. Our ability to anchor what power actually looks and feels like in any one of the seven dimensions in our life—meaningful work, connections with others, self awareness, financial vitality, physical vitality, creative expression, and spiritual connection—provides us the tools for evaluation and expansion of power in any of the other dimensions. We can tap into the experience, the processes, and sensations of authentic power and apply it to other dimensions in our life. Even the simple acknowledgement that we're connected in at least one dimension can keep us from pulling the covers over our head and staying in bed the rest of our lives.

4. Power is a process.

A shift to true power is a process, not a finish line. We don't suddenly get it and then life progresses magically. We don't really ever graduate from this lesson, we just keep learning it in a bigger and bigger context. Because it's a process of unlearning old patterns and healing old wounds, we keep receiving the opportunity to become clearer and clearer about power in our lives.

And because it's a process, it's guaranteed there will be times when we are stuck. We need to allow ourselves to find help in whatever form is comfortable—taking a workshop, seeing a therapist, chanting, calling a friend, journaling, hiking to a mountain top, lighting a candle with a priest, calling in a shaman, moving. We must become aware of our habits and patterns that indicate when we're stuck and make the conscious effort to move. It's a sign of strength not weakness to recognize when we need help.

STORIES OF OWNING IT

Next we present the stories of women who have made the conscious choice to own that they *are* power and to live their lives from that belief. Even when others wanted to derail their plans or place them in the back seat, they discovered the place within that firmly stated "no." When they discovered they were the ones constricting their own lives, these women dug deep to let go of old patterns and unleash their power. None of them would say they set that as their intention, but they all said that owning the knowledge of not just who they are, but also what they are, has been the result. The women in this book own their own Courage Code.

Marsha ✕ Out of the Blue

What happens when you have a perfect life and something suddenly happens, without any real warning, to disrupt and change it? Marsha is a woman who has learned much about power and control. Twice her perfect life changed dramatically overnight and not by her own choosing.

Marsha and her family had what she saw as the perfect life. Her mother was devoted to raising the children and her father was an executive with a corner office and a window. When she was sixteen Marsha's father died suddenly of a heart attack, leaving her mother with young children and the need to find a job after not working outside the home for seventeen years. "My mother went from being an executive wife to one of the girls in the secretarial pool. But she never blinked an eye; she did what she had to do with great courage. She always taught me to play the hand I was dealt; to face reality and get on with it."

Her father's death changed Marsha's views about how much control she had in her own life. Although she had been taught that she could be whatever she wanted to be, "after my father died it was like, ok, I am really not in control of everything. That was a big lesson for me and quite frankly, it has been continually a smart thing to know as an adult. I realized that the only power you have is over yourself—your own attitudes, your own beliefs, your own values and your own behavior. Actually, a better way of putting it is, in the midst of everything else that happens around you, the power you have is how you react or respond."

Years later she was once again living a perfect life. She was settled in a challenging job where she had found her niche. Marsha felt she was making a difference in her community, her teenage son was happy and healthy, and she was remarried to a wonderful man who shared her values and goals. They lived in a beautiful house, in a nice neighborhood, and were respected as community leaders. "We just had this great fun life; in my mind it was the perfect life." Marsha was very content.

Suddenly, however, her life changed dramatically—again, from an external force not of her choosing. Her husband, who held a highly visible and prominent position in the community, came face-to-face with his alcoholism in a very public way. Overnight, their private lives were under the community's and local newspaper's unrelenting microscope. "When all of the public fervor happened I kept thinking, *Wait a minute, I didn't do anything wrong, so why is my life in chaos? Why has my whole life as I know it, my reputation I've worked so hard for, and my place in the community as a leader, changed?"* Marsha struggled with her resentment and fear until she started drawing once again on the lessons she had learned earlier about courage, power, and control. "At first I couldn't get it. Then I realized that as things come up that you don't have control over, you can always go back to that place of figuring out what you do have control over. As I get older the more I realize how little control we really have."

Marsha began digging deeper into her spirituality. "The most courageous thing people can do is face their reality—to stop denying it and accept it. I think the spiritual step is to say that it happened for a reason. The courageous part is to just accept it. I realized I had a choice...the choice to react. It was my choice to harbor resentment against people and against the paper, and I didn't have to do that."

Marsha started taking time everyday for herself, reading inspiring books, and tapping into the support of others. "I have a very busy schedule but quite frankly, when I don't take time for those things I can feel it. I find myself just annoyed by little things. The other day I read something in a memo on my computer and I was wildly furious. I slapped my hand down on the desk, cussed at the top of my lungs, and slammed out the door of my office. And once I got outside I thought, *Whoa, where did that come from? I didn't take my morning time today, did I?"*

For Marsha, power comes from clearly understanding what she has control of in any given situation. "I overcome any fear of the future by saying to myself, *All I can do is the best I can do today. I can't control the outcome but I can control my reaction. That's where my power comes from—my choice of how I will respond to whatever comes my way.*"

Sandra ✗ Singing from the Mountaintop

Some people are understated in expressing who they are. Not Sandra. In all areas of her life—her clothes, house, work, activism, and relationships—there's never any guessing about who she is or what she cares about. Her philosophy for herself and other women is, "If somebody doesn't like me for who I am than they really don't like the real me."

In many ways her life could be viewed as a great contradiction. On one hand, some would say Sandra is extremely selfish. She lives life exactly as she wants, doing what she wants, wearing clothes and colors she likes, and speaking up for what she believes in. And yet, on the other hand, Sandra is also driven by a very unselfish passion to help others. Her life's ambition is to give women shelter, work and beliefs to see themselves as strong and powerful, and to use their power to create a good, peaceful world.

As a child Sandra "never liked doing what I was told to do." Even her mother used to be worried. "She had some concerns that I was a very mixed-up, emotionally disturbed child. Until I went to a psychiatrist who told my mother that I was very well-adjusted and very happy." Later on, however, in her drive to live her life as she wanted, she "thought the way to get independence and freedom was with guys so they could take me places and buy me things." She married early to an older man and had three children, and while her husband was a very nice guy, she didn't like being married at all. "I wanted to change the world and he wanted a house with a circular drive." They divorced after ten years.

Sandra's definition of power and courage is, "Not letting anything stop you. Doing what you feel is the right thing, no matter what." As a mother she courageously stepped up for her children by advocating for their rights as individuals and questioning school policies. "I have gotten in more trouble with a three-letter word than a four-letter...the three-letter word being *Why?*" When her son had an accident at school Sandra questioned the school superintendent about why children were not allowed to play on the grass, which may have prevented the accident. She was told there were concerns about the children hurting the grass. "I told him I have fifty mothers that would be showing up at three o'clock with signs that read 'Pretty Lawns or Broken Limbs' if the policy was not changed. At 2:55 he called and said a new arrangement had been made so the children could now play on the grass. I had exaggerated forty-nine of my mothers, but it worked!"

From an early age Sandra was determined to live a life that would make her happy. "I am not sure if I was confident in my abilities or just knew that I wanted to do what I wanted to do." As result she has created a life she loves. She lives in a rural area on the east coast in a "purple Quonset hut" surrounded by woods and mountains. In the summer she swims in a mountain-fed stream everyday for two hours, "I love water and I swim like a mermaid." She frequently wears purple and buys "sparkly, bubbly clothes." "Today teaching class I had on my purple sparkle hat, my hair is purplish and long." She loves music and organized a Goddess Gospel Choir that she sings in regularly. Sandra is in a very satisfying lesbian relationship, and she surrounds herself with diverse, interesting people. "I love my life. I am surrounded by people I like, doing what I like and I am free and happy. I feel like a goddess because nobody can make me do what is against my principles."

Sandra's passion for living life shows up in her work: running a shelter program for homeless and battered women. "I think it is important because it makes me feel happy and it is doing something towards making the world a better place." Her main message to women is, "Never allow anybody to stop you from doing what you want or being who you are. Basically, we are all very powerful, important, and special. We all deserve to be free and not give our energy or power to those who oppress us."

Debby ✗ Remembering She Can Walk

Real isn't how you're made, said the Skin Horse. It's the thing that happens to you. You become. It takes a long time.

—The Velveteen Rabbit

Debby always loved the book, *The Velveteen Rabbit.* It spoke to her, inspired her and eventually became a guide for her life. It was the metaphor for the transition she knew she needed to make in her life. As she describes it, "I set the intention to become real."

After twenty-five years in a stifling marriage, Debby felt numb, hollow, and voiceless; she felt anything but real. She recalls one afternoon, while shopping laughing and enjoying the company of friends, she was fixated on her watch. Debby was keeping a fretful eye on the time so as to not be late for the preparation of her husband's dinner. Noticing her anxiousness one of her friends said, "You don't have to live this way." Debby's reaction surprised even her. "It occurred to me at that moment that I had forgotten I could leave my marriage. I had lived in a confining relationship so long that I had become ingrained into the patterns of my prison." Her children were grown and out of the house and it dawned on her that she no longer needed to provide for them. Debby realized she had nothing to lose and finally took the first courageous step to get real. She got a job. And that was the start of something big.

As the real Debby began to emerge, she excelled in her job. Her sense of beauty and desire to help other women made her a natural leader in cosmetic sales. And since she was now living on her own following her divorce, her success was providing her the income she needed for her life. "It was amazing to know that I could stand on my own two feet—that I could make choices and even mistakes and everything would be just fine." With each step she took to move out from the self-imposed boundaries of her previous life Debby gained the confidence and skills needed to function in the world. "I felt like I had an invisible tool belt and every time I did something or accomplished something like checking into a hotel by myself for the first time, I added it to my tool belt to use later."

Debby credits her incredible circle of friends with supporting and encouraging her to make the changes necessary. She sees the importance of surrounding herself with people that honor and respect one another. "We get together regularly and share what's going on. We tell each other to 'go for it' and try to inspire and challenge each other to walk through the fire and get through to the other side of fear. When all else fails, we simply share a little wine and a lot of chocolate and that's ok too."

"In the past, I lived my life based on the concept of safety. For fifty years I heard *Don't do that—it's not safe, don't go there—it's not safe, don't see them—they're not safe.* Sometimes I still want to play it safe, but now I know it's just not healthy."

Recently Debby decided to step out of the safety zone again and resigned from her position. She lived in the uncomfortableness of not knowing what was next in her life. It was over six months before she got the revelation that she needed to start her own business helping women do what she has done—get real. Debby hopes her determination to change her life has a ripple effect not just on the women she serves, but on her children as well. "I want to be an example for my daughter to see she has choices."

Unlike Margery William's *The Velveteen Rabbit,* Debby has discovered that transformation doesn't come from a boy or a magic nursery fairy, but from her own courage and determination to be real. "I've discovered I have a voice! And now I'm all about using it in all kinds of ways. I can say 'no' and the world doesn't crumble and I can say 'yes' and create a plan and magic happens."

Geri ✗ Under the Radar

"I can remember the day when I discovered I was a multi-tasker. I thought it was the breakthrough of my life. I can see now that when things move that quickly, when I'm trying to get so much done, that I am actually missing my life. It has taken me a long time to realize this slower pace of just paying attention and doing what is right in front of me—doing one thing at a time is my style. It really is great."

Geri's nickname used to be "Hurricane"—an indication of the speed at which she worked and accomplished. She prided herself in over-achieving and doing four or five things simultaneously. Her approach was rewarded in the outside world with all the finest her very large salary could buy—fabulous home, sporty convertible, luxurious vacations, and a trophy boyfriend. She was ostensively very happy. She had it all. Then she got the eye twitch that wouldn't go away.

When Geri signed up for a meditation class in the hopes of getting the problem under control she never guessed the turn her life would take. The foundation of Buddhist teachings upon which the class was built were all truths she believed, but had never expressed. That simple meditation class took her down the path of studying the Buddhist traditions and changing every aspect of her life.

Geri, like most women, doesn't think of herself or her actions as particularly courageous. "We're all born with natural tendencies. Our whole lives people try to talk us into the 'shoulds' and 'have-tos.' If you don't get cornered by those, you get cornered by what you're good at. That's where I was. But the real task for us is to be who we are literally. The real work of a lifetime is to figure out who I am really. Once I gave myself permission to be who I am, it started to unfold. And it always unfolds in a way that is just perfect. With every shift and deepening of my knowing, I have gotten a lot calmer and healthier with less money." She believes in the Buddhist expression of asking herself to approach life by taking right-action—doing the perfect thing that is called for in the situation regardless of what it might mean to your personal situation.

When Geri moved from a large university town to the inner-city of a large metropolitan area most of her friends and family thought she was nuts. She didn't see herself as crazy or even courageous, but simply taking right-action. "There wasn't any real thinking about it. It was just about doing it. I knew my work was here and I needed to live here. I wanted to create a refuge where people could come and get energy to do the right thing. I don't care what the right thing is—just wherever a person's life is going—to do the right thing. If enough people are doing the right thing, than the world is going to change."

Although she doesn't think about it much, Geri does say that "anyone who stands up for what is, is courageous." And she's had plenty of times to practice that in the unpredictable environment of the inner city. Shortly after she opened the retreat center a guy from the neighborhood starting breaking into people's cars and stealing their books. He would then stand at the front door and sell the books back to them. This went on for awhile until Geri saw him on the corner one day. She went up to him, looked him straight in the eyes, and said, "I need you to take 100 steps from that front door and stop stealing the books—just stop, I need you to stop." And he did.

Geri believes we hold ourselves back in situations like this because we think we have so much to lose. "We have both a right and an obligation to be happy. There is no reason not to do what you want to do."

At the center Geri regularly offers seminars for women starting their own businesses. Many interesting and sustainable businesses have been launched from her approach of helping people find what they love and then seeing how it could be a business that solves someone else's problem. One woman delivers homemade soup chock full of organic vegetables. Together, two women have started a day care. Another has started a clothing business. Geri has witnessed first-hand the power of financial opportunity, "Women's lives change through economic independence and empowerment. It's difficult in this area because there aren't many traditional opportunities so people rely on living off the system. I believe we all want economic independence, sometimes we just don't know how to put it together."

One of the Buddhist teachings that Geri passes on to other women says that no matter what you do, half the people will hate you. "It just doesn't matter, so you might as well just be who you are. Women are under the radar, where all the change really happens. We can get things done. We can start businesses, make money together, and begin to feel useful. And the next thing you know you start to say 'no' to an abusive relationship or stand up for yourself at work and the world begins to change. That's how it will happen, it's going to be the pieces you sweep together. It will be a necklace of the small changes that transforms the look and structure of the system in which we all live. Women have this capacity to change the world."

Suzanne ✕ Walking in Two Different Worlds

Trying to strike a balance and create wholeness takes determination. At age fifty-six Suzanne went back to school to become a massage therapist out of her need to have greater balance in her life. "I feel such joy now. I love my day job, though it is very demanding, and I am also very fulfilled by this other [massage therapy and vibrational healing] part of my life because I can really help other people one-on-one."

When she was in her early twenties and fresh out of college, Suzanne fully expected to have plenty of jobs to choose from. Much to her surprise, she found out there were few opportunities, especially for a woman. "It never occurred to me that I would not be able to do what I wanted to do. So, when I came face-to-face with the real world and experienced such discrimination against women, it was a complete surprise. I didn't really know how to come to terms with it."

She realized that her only course of action in dealing with the reality of the discrimination was to "take a look at all my options and then try to work through what was the most positive thing for me to do at the time. It was really about me taking responsibility for myself." It changed her whole approach to life; she went full circle from believing she could do anything she wanted in her life to questioning those beliefs and then back to a fuller understanding that she was responsible for her own life. "I decided I was not going to let ridicule stop me and I would keep on moving forward without becoming bitter. It was really a time of working that through and kind of coming out at the other end."

Helping her come to terms during that difficult time were friends she met when she began working in the corporate world. Most of the women were older and served as role models to her. They showed her the value of female friendships and about not being judgmental about other people and situations, "They taught me how to celebrate other people's successes and how important it is to work through the issues of envy or jealousy when other people are getting something you want. I learned the more love you send, and the more that comes from your heart, the more that will come back to you." It was a defining lesson for Suzanne.

She continued in her career, moving with opportunities as they presented themselves and finding ways in all situations to give back to others with heart. "Even something as simple as periodically putting a bouquet of flowers in the ladies room. It is amazing what that does. Everyone reacts positively to it. All the women say things like, 'Oh, my gosh, thank you so much. You have no idea what a difference that makes.'" Actions such as these fit Suzanne's belief that "it doesn't have to be grand to impact others and make them feel better."

A few years ago she realized there was another path she wanted to follow. "Making that decision was difficult because it went against a lot of what I had grown up with. I had to start to really look at becoming a healer." It took courage to follow her heart because many people she knew didn't "appreciate or fully understand spirituality and how that can be a part of healing. But there are always situations where we have to reach inside and understand what our own truth is." She now has a full-time corporate job and does massage therapy in the evenings and weekends. Her interest in different types of healing therapies has motivated her to incorporate color, sound, and light into her massage practice.

Following her heart and doing the healing work has taught her a great deal about acting courageously. "One of my greatest fears is what are people going to think about me? That was a big one when my own family and other people would question the areas I was exploring as a healer by saying, 'How can you be dealing with this weird stuff? What are you thinking?' I think those same fears come up working in a large organization—

what are people going to say?"

Suzanne has come to realize that for her to own her power means "really connecting inside to what you know is right for you and then just either standing up for it, speaking it, or doing it." In her day job she acts courageously through the types of projects she undertakes or advocates for. "When I bring up projects having to do with balance or the softer side of things many people make fun of them or try to belittle them. But I believe they're important and the information is important so I am willing to risk making the suggestions. When you know that something is valuable and helpful, and can make a difference in somebody else's life, it is important to continue pursuing it."

The balance she has created in her job choices shows up in many other ways in her life. "I think balance is very important so I try to do things like Tai Chi and meditation. I also have a life outside of either one of my businesses. I enjoy going to the art museum and it never fails to center me and help me balance out. Or I go sit in a garden and even though I live in the city in a townhouse, I surround myself with green by having living plants all around. Anytime we can connect with nature and beauty it is very helpful to creating greater balance in our lives."

Jill ✕ Looking at the Bigger Picture

Looking at Jill's life from the outside, it's easy to see her determination to make deliberate life choices. While those choices have not always made her life an easy one, she is clear that her choices are guided by her strong value for teaching loving kindness. "I'm not holier than thou," says Jill, "but I do know I have a responsibility to teach loving kindness through my actions."

Jill's career choice sprang from this value. She was always interested in business and accounting but when she started her business major she was dismayed there "was no discussion about the common good." As a young girl she had been very involved in Girl Scouts and church groups, and had seen "girls making decisions, not just the boys" and had been exposed to other, more collaborative, types of decision making. "I knew there was another world out there besides traditional business but I didn't know it was nonprofit." She had her first taste of the nonprofit world when she took a class on healthcare administration. "I loved the philosophy of doing good in business *and* doing good for others; it validated my beliefs."

When she graduated the economy was terrible. During a temporary stint as a secretary she was asked to sit in and take notes at a high-level, confidential business meeting. As Jill rode up in an elevator to the conference room she was the lone woman with "all suits, all men." When she stepped out into a plush, elegantly appointed meeting area so different from the dismal surroundings the rest of the company's workforce were stuck in, she was suddenly aware that "this is what I didn't want in life—this eliteness, with no women making decisions. It served as an affirmation for my choice to work in the service sector."

Not long after that she happened to pick up a *Reader's Digest* and came across an eye-opening article on child abuse. Jill soon took a job with a child abuse prevention agency and in her first professional job she felt like she had it all. "There were nurturing, competent women I worked with, we all complemented each other, we were doing important work, and I found my voice for public speaking. That job set me up with the belief that the rest of my work life would be magical."

An added bonus for Jill was being pregnant during that time. "It was a wonderful touch to welcome my daughter into that magical time of my life." As a young mother she appreciated knowing there were agencies helping women and children prevent violence in their lives, "It validated, once again, that my choice to work in nonprofits was a good one."

Several other deliberate choices followed. She married a man who shared her deep values for spiritual connection and loving kindness, and with him, committed to a family mission to gift much of their money. While she says the average philanthropic gift in the U.S. is 2% to 2.5% of income, Jill and her family give "a minimum of 35% up to, at times, 72% of our income. We can do this because my husband is a clergyman and our housing is provided. I come out of a world, professionally, that appreciates giving, and personally, I know how good it feels to make a gift. This congruence in my life contributes to my commitment to be a generous person." Given this generosity one might think that Jill lives with scarcity, yet as she describes it, there is little she lacks, "We live well, travel often, and have everything we need. Pleasures are good...I don't happen to believe money is the root of all evil. I see money simply as a tool and I've just chosen to use this tool differently."

Jill's choice to "do things with the least impact on others and the environment" has not always been easy. "When times have been difficult I've questioned this choice and thought, *This is stupid!* But time brings me back. Time goes on and I get perspective on how important this choice is to me." She also turns to her faith for the grounding she needs. "From my years teaching Sunday school I've found it's the clearest thing I can do to teach love and acceptance. It keeps me honest and accountable, and keeps me going. It keeps me centered." Seeing the impact on her daughter also keeps her focused, "My daughter is a socially responsible adult and this affirms our path."

Recalling the women in her life who have impacted and supported her also helps Jill make choices that work for her. "There have been so many cool women, even women I didn't know." Growing up, she was influenced by the strength of her grandmothers and mother, as well as by the important role of the women in her community, "I saw the church being run by women, just like the band boosters, Girl Scouts, and other groups." As a young adult she discovered women's history which opened her eyes to the significant contributions of unnamed and named women. As a result Jill says, "I believe in women because they have more opportunities to be in touch with all parts of their being and have greater ability to integrate their whole self."

Joanna ✕ The Snake Charmer

A snake, for many, is one of the surest triggers of fear and trepidation. For Joanna, however, a snake has come to symbolize something very different: transformation, life, and power.

As a young woman in the 1970s she was very involved in and influenced by the feminist movement, "I have been very much a woman, like others of my generation, who put a lot of male energy—action, focus on a career—into my life." She thought she knew what feminine power was and built a life that included being a clinical social worker, peace activist, and community volunteer. And while she also practiced yoga, meditation, and Native American spirituality, she admits her focus was still on doing and achieving.

All that changed when Joanna was diagnosed with breast cancer. Undergoing radiation and chemotherapy "has called me to my courage and has called me to step into my power—the power of feminine receptivity. It is a different kind of power, the willingness to surrender to nurturing, listening to my need for help, and accepting help. It is not the power of going out there and being assertive which is the male energy I was so used to putting out."

Joanna's cancer led her to new wisdom about her feminine side, a side she thought she understood but realized she didn't. "What I had to learn through my cancer was how to be more receptive to receiving love. I began to look at everything symbolically; my cancer is in my left breast, the place that represents nourishment, giving and receiving nourishment—our feminine side. So I learned I needed to surrender to letting people help me more, asking for more help."

For her first chemo session she had a friend meet her at the treatment site. Afterwards, they went home separately. Joanna went to her much-loved ceramics class, but halfway through the class she became desperately ill. Joanna's fellow sculptors helped her home as she sobbed through the waves of nausea. "It was a very important lesson for me about my ability to ask for help. On one hand, I was saying it's okay; if someone called me I would certainly respond happily to their call for help. But that little voice inside was also saying, *oh, they're going to be upset with me for asking for help.* I had to surrender to my need for help, the realization I couldn't do it alone, and be truly receptive to the nurturing that was being offered." For her following treatments she always asked someone to be with her during the treatment and then take her home.

Once chemotherapy began Joanna realized she needed help

with the daily stuff of life: housecleaning, yard work, and so on. One day she arrived home and, unbeknownst to her, two friends had shown up and quietly went about mulching her gardens. Again she was challenged to simply accept their help, "I had to learn how to graciously receive which is the deepest power of the feminine that was calling to me. It is okay for me to receive help and not have to do something in response. I don't have to think any longer, I will have do to something in return for them...I just have to receive their gift."

Joanna's deep friendships with the women in her ceramics class served as an anchor since she was diagnosed with cancer. The opportunity to express herself through clay gave rise to a powerful symbol of transformation and healing. For some time the cobra snake had had meaning for her, and one day Joanna had a powerful dream about a cobra. In pondering the message of her dream she began to understand that cobras know how to work with poison, and as such, she could tap into the cobra's knowledge for healing. She also realized she could be the snake charmer in control of the cobra. Her dream moved her to craft a cobra sculpture which has served to inspire her and other women healing from cancer.

In thinking about the lessons gained from her illness Joanna believes all women benefit from "greater balance between male and female energy. There is a fine line. You have to read the intuition between action and non-action. When do you need to act and when do you not need to act? It is about truly trusting that in the being and receiving things will come to us and be okay. It is that basic—I am going to be okay. Our greatest challenge is to claim that receptive part of ourselves which is the inner listening."

Kate ✗ Moving Forward

"Courage is the strength to be responsible for yourself. It is knowing what you want and where you need to be, and taking the risks to get there. It's about keeping moving."

Kate is familiar with taking risks and doing what needs to be done. As a single parent at twenty-one, on welfare, and raising her daughter alone, she was clear about what she wanted. Her sole priority was being an active parent and being there for her child no matter what it took.

Kate's parenting goal guided the decisions she made about jobs she took and where she put her time and energy. At one point she drove a school bus so she could be there when her daughter got home from school. She decided to go back to school to be a social worker so she could be a good role model for her child. Later on when she left her social work job to get a graduate degree in business she created a schedule that allowed her to be home everyday at 3:00 pm to meet her daughter's school bus. Parenting always deeply fulfilled her and she willingly made personal and professional decisions with her daughter in mind. "Jobs can come and go and careers change. But in truth all that is superfluous to parenting."

But it wasn't always easy. "Because I was not into climbing up career ladders and getting promoted I experienced a lot of difficult financial issues." Kate also struggled with trying to find balance in giving to her child and giving to herself. "My mom used to be the kind of person who always took the bad end of the meat or just the inferior thing in any situation. I think that modeled that she was not worthy or she did not see her own worth. So I wanted to have a different impact by standing up for myself in front of my daughter, *and* by letting her see me standing up for her."

Kate is enjoying the freedom she has now that her daughter is 25 years old and living a happy, independent life in another state, "I can go home after work and eat a bowl of cereal for dinner and not feel guilty. I can work and play as hard as I want... I feel like I'm on vacation." She does miss her days of active parenting, though. "In many ways even though I enjoy and am very, very involved in my job and don't feel the pressure now that I did when my daughter was with me, things in my life just don't have the same importance as parenting did. The relationship between a parent and a child and all you go through with them is mostly wonderful stuff and very important, whether it's cutting teeth, getting them through elementary school, or helping them on the soccer team."

Never one to stand still Kate's life continues to move forward as her priorities have shifted. "You know moving forward has a lot to do with what your current priority is. I think that as priorities change your life situation changes. When I was parenting my priorities were around that. Now one of my biggest objectives is to make as much money as I can so I have more choices in the future." To that end she has thrown herself into her job working in higher education, and building up her real estate assets. As with her parenting choices, Kate is willingly and with clarity making choices that move her forward in line with this priority. "I look at somebody like a friend of mine who just quit her fulltime job and is now working for herself. That's an option for me to do as well, but I am choosing not to do that because I have other priorities right now."

Kate is a big advocate for tapping into intuition when moving forward. "I think it is really important to pay attention to your intuition and what your gut is telling you. If your first instinct is to take action, then don't second guess or rationalize yourself out of it." To be clearer about what her intuition is saying she turns to quiet time and physical exercise. "It keeps my energy more balanced and is a good way to blow off steam." Astrology is also important to her, "My chart shows I am always looking forward, always looking for tomorrow." She combines her belief in astrology with skills in project management, "I just keep moving the ball forward, constantly moving and advancing. Sometimes it's a slow, agonizing process. But to me, it's not okay to stay stagnant."

Lisa ✕ Cliff Jumping

Lisa uses a question to guide her life: *Ok, if everything happens for a reason, then what can I learn from this challenge?* She's a therapist who, in recent years, reinvented her life and her practice to include eco-psychology, the study of our human connection to earth and nature. It wasn't easy for Lisa to close her traditional therapy practice and relocate halfway across the country to start over. But then again, Lisa is no stranger to the work of going deep within to find her truth and then acting on it.

In the eighth grade Lisa was diagnosed with scoliosis. For four years she wore a back brace and neck collar twenty-three hours a day. While other young women were learning how to flirt and enjoy attention from others, Lisa was forced to learn deeper lessons of resiliency and moving beyond adversity. "My mother kept saying, 'This is going to make you a stronger person.' I didn't want to hear that. I didn't want to be a stronger person. I just wanted to be a teenager like everyone else." The self-doubts that came along with being different showed Lisa how important it was to go within, listen to her thoughts, and determine which were coming from her head and which from her heart. This discernment has served her well and has allowed her to stay connected to her truth even in times of trauma.

"One day I came home from school and the field next to our house with a big sledding hill had been leveled. The bulldozers had moved in and just plowed everything under to begin construction of a new subdivision. Even at that age I was so distraught over the carelessness with the earth and other living beings." Lisa knew that she couldn't pretend the pain in her heart would just go away so she looked for the lesson in the hardship and uncovered her profound connection with the earth. She made the decision to enroll in college out west so she could be surrounded by mountains and live amidst their beauty.

In later years, as her marriage was ending, Lisa went back to her core question *What am I supposed to learn?* "I was depressed a lot. I just had this attitude that it is too hard. I do all this work to try to figure it out and it just gets hard again. I realized that carrying around that attitude was the meanest thing I could to do myself. With my divorce, I think I just got bored with thinking that way." So Lisa got real with herself. She went back to asking the important questions like *What do I love? What am I passionate about? What is my purpose?*

The answers came slowly, but she soon realized that they were all pointing in the direction of understanding our connections with nature. "I had to give myself permission to do my work in the way my intuition was telling me to." She began by facilitating Earth Walks, opening a sacred time for people to connect with nature and hear the truth that is reflected in the natural world. At first only one or two people would show up, but she kept putting her passion out there. Soon there were seven, then ten, and it just continued to grow. Today she facilitates workshops and individual sessions that harness the healing power of nature and allows individuals to express their feelings about our earth.

Through her own journey Lisa has been able to help others appreciate and love themselves even in the midst of self-doubt. "The fear I run up against most often is self-doubt. *Can I really do this? Am I able?* It has helped me to notice it, be aware of it, and learn to have compassion for myself when I'm in it. But nowhere does it say I have to stay there!"

Lisa feels especially drawn to the red rock desert of Utah where she regularly challenges her physical, mental, emotional, and spiritual bodies through wilderness canoeing. "I have a favorite spot—a cliff with a twenty-foot drop into a pool of water. I love to stand on that edge and, before the jump, focus my attention on the fear that is coursing through my body. Those moments teach me to be aware and amazed with the total experience of fear and doubt and compassion. But sooner or later, I have to jump."

It's Yours ✕ Use It

It's Yours ✕ Use It

*Be prepared—when you finally summon the courage to cast a vote for
yourself, you can expect obstacles. The whole world will rise up to tell you
who you cannot become and what you cannot do. Those around you will
be threatened as you exceed the limited expectations they've always
had for you.*

O. WINFREY

O‍K, LET'S BE TRUTHFUL. When you look at your day, did you
really do anything that even comes close to being courageous?
Did you run into a burning building to rescue a screaming child?
Did you give it all you have and climb a mountain? Perhaps you
ran onto a battlefield and lifted your friend out of harm's way—
yeah right!

More than likely you got up this morning, and even though
you were dead tired, you greeted your kids with a warm smile.
Perhaps you directly and respectfully addressed a difficult issue
with someone. Maybe you followed through on registering for a
class that you knew was important for you despite other
demands and responsibilities in your life. Or maybe you suggested a new, collaborative approach to a thorny problem at

work. If you did anything similar to these acts, you did indeed exhibit courage.

Why don't we recognize these less-than-valorous acts as courageous? We each demonstrate it every day. And yet, we do not acknowledge it, understand it, and especially do not honor it. Courage: the word can be both inspiring and diminishing because we don't see ourselves in it. Courage. It's a larger-than-life word, suggesting bold acts of heroics—acts that seem to have little to do with our everyday lives.

THE OLD CODE

Our societal definition of courage has grown over the centuries to demand larger and larger acts of valor. Those who are seen as courageous are those who brave the elements to save another, those who go to war from a sense of duty, and those who single-handedly take on the system to fight for change. While there is no denying that all these acts require courage, it seems that our current definition is limited and limiting.

Courage has evolved into meaning putting your life on the line—your physical life. It's associated with the machismo of bravery, or steadfastness that requires a stiff upper lip, or perhaps a strict denial of fear. In the current Code, courage is about strength and firmness. Competition, a need to prove one's self, and winning at all costs has distorted this word to such a level that women rarely connect with it or use it to describe themselves. We find we're outside the paradigm with a sense of diminishment of ourselves and the quiet acts of courage we routinely display.

SHUTTING DOWN OUR COURAGE

We all feel the ways in which society diminishes and devalues the feminine face of courage. At the same time we, as women, undervalue our own courage. In interviewing the women in this book we found there are four common ways in which we discount our acts of heart, thereby keeping us in line with society's expectations and from seeing ourselves as courageous.

1. It wasn't courage, I had to do it.

Of all the responses to questions about the acts of courage women display in their lives the one that surfaced most consistently was this: In interview after interview, women said they felt that changing careers, relationships, or lifestyles was not necessarily courageous, just what they felt they had to do. It wasn't that they did these things impulsively or without thought, it was just that they felt there was no valid reason for entertaining the option *not* to.

They seem to be saying that if they jumped off a bridge to save a person from drowning—now *that* would be courageous; but saving their own life from a metaphorical drowning, well, that was no big deal. Many discussed having to get beyond feelings of selfishness or guilt in order to take the action required to reclaim or save their life.

Yet, even when a change disrupted their families or careers, their new way of living felt so right that these women often forgot the ring of fear they passed through in order to get their new life. It's important to see these acts as courage, to codify them as courage, and to acknowledge that we are courageous in those moments so we don't diminish our accomplishments and forget we chose to take action.

2. If I'm not courageous 24/7, then I'm not courageous at all. As part of believing there is a gold standard of courage we compare ourselves to others and judge ourselves harshly if we feel we don't measure up. We look at Eleanor Roosevelt, Dana Reeve, or Rosa Parks and think that courage was probably a reflexive response for them—something they never had to think about or even consider. We hold ourselves up to their achievements and our lives pale in comparison.

Many of the women we interviewed hesitated to define

themselves as courageous because they have moments in their lives when they choose not to speak from their heart or choose not to confront someone directly. We discount ourselves when we don't acknowledge there is a right time to take a courageous step because we believe courage has to be instanteous. We must give ourselves permission to take the time needed to come to peace with the possible ramifications of courageous actions; otherwise, we set a standard for ourselves that is impossible to meet and is destructive to our selves.

Our tendency to live in the past can also be limiting. Even women who have exhibited tremendous courage by opening a business or leaving a marriage hesitated to describe themselves as courageous because they're still beating themselves up with the memory that they didn't stand up to the bully in the fourth grade. This all or nothing approach to courage shows that women don't cut themselves any slack.

Our perfectionism also affects our view of being courageous. We use our perceived failings to feel bad about ourselves over and over again. Like self-determination and power, courage has no finish line. We don't magically get to a place where we're acting with heart in every moment and then win a medal. It takes deep healing, dedicated connection to one's Self, and letting go of others' expectations to bring us to a place of peace with our own courage. Every step along the way should remind us of our naturally courageous nature we are reclaiming. By affirming each courageous step, we affirm our wholeness.

3. If I'm courageous, then I'll be in the spotlight.

We're not likely to gain much media attention when we act in our own best interest, so there's very little chance that most of us will end up center stage or on the local news. However, when we choose not to acknowledge our acts of courage publicly (this could just mean with our friends) we reinforce the paradigm of the feminine needing to play the supporting or secondary role.

Some of the women we talked to admitted that it was difficult to describe themselves as courageous because at a deep level they were still aware of the admonishment that they *should be seen and not heard.* Many could remember the moments when they heard from parents, teachers, and church leaders: *Sit down, be quiet, and smile pretty. Don't be so full of yourself.* We have to work consciously to get beyond this strong indoctrination. The underlying message is that the other gender is more deserving of speaking, acting, and leading. Claiming our courage and seeing ourselves and other women as courageous helps dispel the myth that it is the birthright of only one gender.

4. It feels like a sacrifice—not courage.

Sadly, women as connectors and collaborators often feel the affects of courage as disruptions and loss. If we don't see the act of confronting an addicted parent as courage, we are destined to see it as a sacrifice of the relationship. When we focus on what is lost, instead of what is gained, we fall quickly into victimhood and disempowerment. The perceived sacrifice is that the courageous act will change everything, including us. Many of us have lived so long in a place of imbalance and dis-ease that we're actually comfortable being there. It certainly is easier to stay where we know what will happen, even if it is destructive.

Several women shared emotional stories of acting from their heart which subsequently involved confrontation or leaving a relationship, job, or location. Today, they describe themselves as courageous because they focus on how they have grown because of it, not on what they have given up or lost. When we do what is in our highest good, it is always in the highest good for all. No one ever relinquished their abusive power by having us stay there and take it.

Dan Pallotta, visionary and creator of The AIDS Ride and 3-Day Cancer Walk, put it succinctly when he said, "When it is not an option for someone to dislike you, you are left with very few options. And one of the options you are sure to have eliminated is staying true to your heart." When we act from our heart there will be life changes *and* it is likely that there will be losses. The over-dramatization that comes when we project that *everything* will change can be a convenient barrier to moving forward. The truth is, when we acknowledge our courageous action, the biggest change occurs within us—mentally, emotionally, and spiritually.

A NEW CODE

The root of the word courage is from the Old French "with heart." Its original meaning was literally *to* "act with heart." In her inspiring book, *Courage: The Heart and Spirit of Every Woman,* Sandra Ford Walston reminds us that "in earlier times, courage meant mental or moral strength to venture, to persevere, and to withstand danger, fear, or difficulty." What a difference this is from the definition that taunts us into believing that might means right.

The feminine face of courage is rarely acknowledged or pursued. The face of courage that acts from heart, is about putting your life on the line—your real life, your essential authentic Self, and that goes far beyond your physical self.

Today's media doesn't cover stories of women who have had the courage to be open and honest in the midst of a relationship conflict or who have bravely worked to create a community committed to supporting all members' growth. Aside from the entertainment value in current network programming, society doesn't focus much attention on the courageous act of following your gut, instinct, or higher guidance. As Walston points out, "the strong woman concept reflects the limits of progress for women in the twenty-first century. Rather than seeing strength and courage as a part of the gentle fabric and soul of any woman, [the strong woman] depicts courage as unusual, atypical, and usually with a masculine bravado."

It is this courage, "from the gentle fabric," that is required of each of us if we are to stay connected to authentic power. If power is what we *are,* than courage is what it takes to be that— what it takes to be full of power.

Courage is the action, the verb that is required of us to live from our authentic Self. And when we exhibit courage, when we take action from our heart the result is authentic power. The process is circular, not linear. As we grow more deeply power-ful, we access more of our courage (more of our heart) which allows us to take the right action that will bring us to an even deeper connection with our power.

The opposite of courage is not fear, it is inaction. When we are *dis*couraged, or *un*courageous, we feel stuck, unable to move, unable to take action. In this state, we're not acting from or even accessing our heart. We say we're in fear, which is simply the opposite of love. When we're in fear we're mentally listing all the reasons why we don't feel we're capable or worthy of love.

We use fear as the reason why we can't act. Fear of rejection, abandonment, being noticed or ignored, disappointing others, and even fear of our own rage keep us from loving ourselves and others fully enough to take the right action, to be courageous. Courage is the call for *an act of love.*

A FEMININE CODE OF COURAGE

We've all done something courageous in our lives. Whether it's wearing a short skirt to school in defiance of our mother, taking a belly dancing class, or balancing our checkbook, as women, we know about routine courage.

It takes courage to follow our inner compass—courage to take a stand, make a change, speak our truth, envision a new reality. When we do, we connect with the authentic power that resides within and it allows us to birth a new way of being powerful in the world. As author Salman Rushdie puts it, "Our lives teach us who we are."

Sometimes, speaking out at a meeting, telling the boss no,

telling the children no, can literally feel like we're putting our life on the line. The very real possibility exists that we'll lose our job, our position, or our relationship. It's in those times that we need to recall our courageous nature, *Hey, I've lived through platform shoes, haven't I?* and choose to save our own lives.

One of our interviewees expressed it beautifully when she came to the realization that her relationship needed to end, and yet, her internal dialogue was conflicted. "I knew choosing for my life meant I was going to have to leave. I didn't want to hurt him, but I couldn't hurt me either." We're conditioned as women to always think of the other person first. And this admirable trait allows women to be strong team builders, potent negotiators and miraculous leaders.

However, when that consideration of others is out of balance we shift from collaboration to simply peace-keeping. The problem with smoothing things over and avoiding conflict is not just that we miss the opportunity for some really juicy dialogue, but that we've stuffed our feelings and have shut down our voices.

Women bring their empowered feminine gifts to the courage table in a way that is desperately needed today. Women see the value in networks, connections, and building bridges rather than blowing them up. Because of this we understand the need to see the larger picture, which includes many points of view, and use this approach to solve problems in our communities and in our world.

The feminine intuitive approach of listening to inner wisdom is a radar that allows women to cut through the immaterial and get to the inclusive visioning that is needed for the betterment of all. Women need to see their everyday acts of heart as courage. They need to appreciate and acknowledge it in themselves and in others because it connects each of us with our power. We need courage. We need to act with heart because we will lead the change in the world without the typical fanfare that comes from heroics, but with the quiet, powerful dignity that comes from love.

USING THE NEW CODE

The courageous acts we've heard about from the women we interviewed were actions within their everyday lives. They were acts of putting their life on the line, their real life, their authentic life. They were acts without fanfare. Every time a woman stepped up to living courageously from this place of authenticity she connected more and more with her true power.

When we choose to act with courage we open the floodgates to our authenticity. Flexing our courage muscle and using our authentic voices in one situation not only encourages us to use it elsewhere it our lives, it actually catalyzes those opportunities.

What can we expect when we act with heart and begin to use our courage? For everyone it's different; however, we can count on three characteristics of courage that are overarching for all.

1. Courage has many faces.

There are as many courageous actions as there are situations in our lives. We each have our old Courage Code that holds us back and keeps us bound that we need to break. Some of the women we interviewed shared that they felt courageous in their careers, but needed reminding that they could also speak from their heart in their relationships. Others felt their relationships were on track, but were having a difficult time facing their financial picture. What is easy for one requires courage for another. One of the important components of the new Courage Code is that there are many faces of courage—all of them important and all of them valid expressions of courage. When we understand this we take an important step in accepting ourselves and others as they are.

2. Courage comes from within.

Courage is an outward expression of heart and spirit. Those who know courage know themselves. It doesn't mean they are never afraid or that their knees don't knock when they're about to embark on something that will be difficult. It does mean they know and trust that no matter what happens in the external world as a result of their actions that internally they will be fine. They know that nothing can truly hurt them when they act from the place of asking, *What is in the best and highest good for all?*

3. Courageous acts can be seemingly small and quiet.

Oftentimes courage is the mouse that roars. It may seem like the dramatic exit is an act of courage, but the old adage "all show and no go," sometimes applies to these kinds of displays. If courage is to act with heart, then it means we look for ways to express our courage that includes making a move, or challenging behavior—all coming from a place of love and respect for others as well as ourselves. Courage can be as simple and elegant as "No, thank you."

STORIES OF USING IT

The following are stories from women who have stepped up and answered the call from their hearts. These are remarkable women doing remarkable things. And yet they are as common as your next-door neighbor. They are living their lives—fully, completely, courageously and they are experiencing the same bumps along the way that you do. They don't have all the an-swers or even some fast-track to courage, they just make the conscious choice to act from their hearts.

Debbie ✕ Providing a New Model

"Courage is the ability to believe in yourself and then be willing to take risks to act on your beliefs."

Courage is a topic Debbie has thought about often and, in her personal and professional lives, she has demonstrated it countless times.

She was "lucky to have been in a family that instilled great acceptance and unconditional love." As a girl growing up with brothers, Debbie's parents gave her the same messages of encouragement as they did the boys. "I was very fortunate I never heard that somehow as a girl I couldn't do something. I was always encouraged to dream, take risks, and have courage." She credits this early foundation of love and support as the source of the courage she has drawn from throughout her life. "I received a real gift from my parents in terms of having confidence in myself."

This confidence is also accompanied by a deep conviction about her role in making a difference in the world. Her choice to major in social work in college was based on a desire to help people. So a life path of serving others was what she expected. What wasn't expected were the twists and turns her path would take and how much courage she would be called on to use.

It started with an issue in her community that Debbie believed was important. She got involved locally, advocating for a new facility to better deliver medical care to low-income seniors. She was young, only 24 years old, still a graduate student, and when she decided to take on the fight she was quickly thrust into the political arena. It was in the early 70s and "women of any age were not that much involved in politics." Her opponent referred to her as "the young broad running against me." Debbie's winning leap into politics was a bold, risky move. "It was an eye-opening experience and sort of a high-risk kind of thing to be doing. It really took a combination of believing in myself and what I wanted to do, and then being willing to risk failure. I think that is a very important part of having courage— that you are willing to believe enough in what you are doing and who you are, and be willing to risk failing."

Since then Debbie has had a steady stream of wins and successes, each requiring her to act with even greater courage. Her current role in the U.S. Senate requires her to "step up everyday, make decisions and use my personal power in some way." This past year she was called upon to make a difficult decision in terms of her stand on a major issue. Debbie took a position "a significant minority position" that required her to "take a deep breath and focus on what was really important to me and what I believe in. I just felt I needed to go with the facts as I saw them and my personal belief in values around that decision." Making the decision to take a stand against the war in Iraq was not easy, nor was the moment she voiced her vote. Yet, despite the pressure she felt she knew in her heart she made the best choice.

She has often felt the pressure—and delight—of being the first woman to hold many of her positions. Debbie sees her pioneering role as providing a new model for other women. "I think I have helped other women define what power and courage look like. I hope my presence in the Senate has given other women permission to want to do the same thing and to do things others may tell them they can't. I think the visual piece is so important, whether a woman is heading a business or a university, holding a political office, or playing basketball in the Final Four. The visual of other women in those places gives the message to girls and other women that they can strive to be the best they can be."

At times the need for her to step up to make tough decisions and take courageous action is taxing. Her work days are long and the issues she deals with are complex. "It's essential not to lose sight of what's important in the craziness of each day. And it's not as if I don't have the same kinds of questioning and self doubts that everybody else has—I do. I have learned to have the courage to press beyond those fears and to just keep going. Still, it's an ongoing work in progress to stay courageous." To this end Debbie takes some daily quiet time to think, along with spending time in prayer and meditation to "clear my mind and focus on what is important."

Something that is very important to her is setting an example for her daughter. "I hope that I have done that by just trying to live my life with self-determination and courage and also by encouraging my daughter to do the same thing. I want to send the message that she can be whatever she wants to be, not by just saying it, but by demonstrating that through my own life. I think it's very important to do that and to constantly be as encouraging as possible in whatever it is our children, boys or girls, are interested in. We need them to know that we believe in their ability to make good choices and to be there in terms of living the right values. It is more about how we live our lives than what we say."

Bethany ✕ The Power of a Vision

"Every single day amazing things happen to me. I am always amazed, but never surprised."

When you meet Bethany it's like meeting a young Katherine Hepburn. She's a statuesque woman and carries herself with a compelling combination of poise and power. But if you had met her even three years ago, you would have noticed something very different.

"I had two emotions back then—anger and not anger. Even though I had been in therapy regarding my abusive father, I never stopped fighting—fighting him and fighting the feeling that I was powerless."

Bethany has always been determined to make something of her life. She put herself through college and then dental school. The fight kept her going. After working with another dentist for a short time, she left to start her own practice, all the while being haunted by her anger. She was depressed, lethargic, and burned out. Because she had no energy she thought that maybe she was in the wrong career. So what happened to create such a dramatic difference in Bethany's life? She attended a visioning seminar for dental practices and realized that she had the power to create her life. "I saw I had a choice to envision a different kind of life for myself and I leapt at it!"

Realizing her depression and life chaos were simply other expressions of her anger, she envisioned a life of peace and calm, regardless of the circumstances. "When I realized that my anger was about rebelling against authority and how it paralleled my anger with my father, I knew I had a choice to react differently. I couldn't change the abuse, but I could change how I interpreted it." She began working one-on-one with a world-class consultant and crafting a vision plan for her new dental practice, the building, and the staff to support it. Soon her energy was picking up and the chaos in her life was leveling off.

When she identified exactly want she wanted a funny thing happened. It began to appear. She found the perfect piece of wooded property that would allow her to build amongst the soothing trees. It was even priced reasonably. Although her friends and family told her she'd never come up with the 25% down needed for the construction loan, Bethany didn't blink. She bought the property knowing somehow it would all work out. The next year a manufacturing plant went in across the street from her vacant land and upgraded the area with water and sewers. Her land appreciated seven-fold and she had the equity to begin building.

Bethany's next challenge was communicating her vision to her work team. She knew it wasn't going to be easy. Even though her practice philosophy was now aligned with her own values, she knew some of the team would not be comfortable with the changes. Bethany worked hard at communicating the vision clearly. Tapping into her natural leadership style, she listened respectfully to each person's opinions. It wasn't about convincing others that she was right, or trying to control them into operating as she did. Bethany laid out her vision and asked if anyone wanted to join her in creating it. It was important to her that the team members realized they had a choice. She never wanted anyone to feel powerless in the situation. Each person made their own decision in their own time—some stayed, some didn't, but the new team was committed to making the practice something special.

Bethany inspires confidence and contentment in her team because she found those two things within herself. To claim her power she continues to move courageously through her emotional issues from her childhood. She realizes it's an ongoing process that reaps great rewards. "Now I know that I am powerful in ways my father will never be. To let me be empowered was a very scary thing for him, too scary. He had to tell me what to think and do and how to act. That's not power. True power is having the self confidence to let others be powerful."

Today the smiling team—they are in the business of smiles after all—work side-by-side to provide quality dental care. Bethany has grown into a leader who is able to be honest and direct. "I feel it's my job to lead them to their own power. They can solve their own problems, they know how to resolve conflicts, and can make decisions without asking. My role is making sure they have the things they need to do that."

When Bethany envisions the future of her practice what does she see? "I want to be the leader who is running behind the pack, with everyone ahead of me. I'm smiling and saying, *I'm their leader.*"

Barbara ✕ Working for the Best of Everyone

It never occurred to Barbara to not be courageous. Looking back on her life she sees that the choices she made and the actions she took were founded in her strong sense of power. Barbara was only the third person in her family to finish college. It was her grandmother, an anchor for her life, who instilled in Barbara the absolute determination to complete her education. "One of the things she would say is: *When* you go away to school... it was never *if*. So I grew up believing I would."

Barbara initially went to college on an athletic scholarship, but was injured early in her sports career. Since this occurred before the passing of Title IX, she, like other female athletes who could not perform, was dropped from the scholarship program. Barbara came home and found a lucrative summer job, but didn't let the money tempt her away from accomplishing her educational goal. She chose a university several states away where no one knew her and began anew. With the help of her family and the income from two jobs, she completed her education. "That was really a turning point for me to say, *Not only am I going to finish college, but I really want to think about the mark I can leave.*"

Drawn to working with young people, Barbara began a mentoring program for the girls who attended an after-school program in her community. Soon the word was out that Barbara was eager and willing to make things happen. People asked her to help with different functions and programs and she always said yes. "Sometimes I didn't know what to do, but I listened and watched. I found assistance from other women who would help me. Then I started to hear this whole script that I was good with young people, especially girls. Because I was good at it people wanted me to stay. But I knew I wanted more in my life, I knew I wanted to have a position of authority and make the decisions." So Barbara didn't take others' advice, instead she went on to complete her master's degree. The decision catapulted her into the sphere of nonprofit management and a career of making decisions and leaving a mark.

Not every decision was an easy one. When her son was young Barbara and her husband relocated so he could accept an executive position with his firm. She knew then her marriage was not going to survive. It was difficult, in a new city and state, to tell her husband their marriage wasn't working and that she needed to leave. But Barbara knew it was the best thing for her and her son. "My ex-husband was very angry with me for a long time. But eventually I went to him and told him we needed to figure out how we could become civil for the sake of our son. To this day he tells me that it took a lot of courage to speak up to him like that. But he could see it in my eyes that I was determined and he knew he had to work through his anger."

When Barbara accepted the leadership of a large YWCA program in an urban setting, she was surprised to learn that the program was a million dollars in debt. Her determination to turn the program around meant that the job demanded her attention almost 24 hours a day, 7 days a week. Not an easy schedule to juggle for a single mother with a pre-teen. Her courage and determination paid off. "My ex-husband and new his wife were fabulous. They were my biggest champions in this. They knew this work was important to me and we all knew our son needed both his father and his mother. So we made it work." Working together for everyone's good became a skill Barbara and her ex would have to cash in on again when she was offered a challenging opportunity out of state. Not wanting to uproot their son during his high school years, they decided it would be best if he moved in with his father. At first, Barbara's mother didn't quite understand how she could leave her child. But as Barbara said, "I didn't leave him in a basket on some doorstep. He was with his dad." She believes the courage it took for her to pack up and move across the country helped build her character, as well as her skills and expertise.

Since that move Barbara has had the opportunity to facilitate the growth and expansion of several organizations; opportunities that required her to move outside her comfort zone to take on something different. "My friends call me a gypsy— packing up and moving when opportunities presented themselves. I have found that I had to move out of my safety zone. When I feel things becoming comfortable, I know it was time for me to move and stretch again."

One thing is always constant—Barbara's passion for helping women. Today, she feels it is more important than ever, in both her professional and personal life, to support other women. "I'm putting my money down where my passion lies. That is with women. Looking at the bigger picture I see how I can use my money to change policy by choosing where I donate. In our household our philanthropy supports education and women. I've been remarried now for eight years and one of the things my husband says is that he is a better feminist now because of me."

Even though she loves her work and is grateful for the opportunity to interact with women all around the state, the country and world, Barbara has a sense there is something more for her to discover about her niche in the world. "My friends tell me all the time that what I do is a perfect fit, but I don't feel that way. I still feel there is more of *me* to find."

Melanie ✕ Opening the Cage Door

Cages come in all sizes and Melanie has figuratively known many of them. Through it all she has maintained a big vision for freeing herself and others from limitations and constraints.

As a young girl growing up in a rural area Melanie sensed she would grow beyond the limits of her life, "When I was a little kid I would walk around and think there was probably a bigger world out there." Her personal mission to help others started early. One of her brothers was blind and attended a special school where Melanie first became aware of the struggles faced by disabled people. From that time on she wanted to do something to assist others in need. "My high school counselor said I was the leader of the pack when it came to giving a voice to someone's issues. People came to me when they couldn't say things for themselves."

In her desire to fight for others' freedom and dignity she became a bit of a rabble-rouser. She organized the first protest rally against the Vietnam War in her small town, "I was always in trouble because I was organizing these groups and protests." Her view of other people was different than most and she was not afraid to speak up in support of their right to choose.

Melanie knew of a wheelchair-bound man who wanted to be independent. "He especially wanted to go fishing, but at the time our town did not have handicap accessible places for him. I would see him struggling to push his wheelchair to the water where he could fish. I approached a member of the city council about making the boardwalks leading to the water more accessible to the disabled. I was told they 'didn't want those people on the pier. What if they fell off?' and I said, 'Well, if they fall off that is their choice.'" Melanie did not back down and, needless to say, the town got a boardwalk.

After many years fighting for others' personal freedom and respect Melanie found herself in a marriage where neither freedom nor respect existed. She felt as if she were trapped in a cage. It took tremendous courage, but eventually she realized she had to leave in order to survive. Melanie fled to the east coast to the safety of a woman's shelter and group. "It may be safe to stay confined, but we have to step outside our comfort zone."

As Melanie began talking with others in her women's group she encountered a world she never knew existed. "It was very bizarre; here I am, a sheltered woman from a very small town, never knowing there were women with such rough lives and so many were living on the streets." She learned important lessons from the homeless women and saw they were not too much different from her. "I realized they were just people—real people, just like me, who were children once with hopes and dreams who didn't want to grow up to live in controlling, abusive relationships."

This experience was a turning point in her life and fueled her passion for working with women and the homeless. "I knew I wanted to use my personal experiences to assist other women in order to feel I was fulfilling my own purpose. I met women while I was traveling who were doing these magnificent things and I didn't want to ever feel caged anymore. I felt a new sense of purpose; I wanted to be the one who helped."

Her travels later took her to Salt Lake City where she volunteered for a soup kitchen, affirming her sense of connection with the homeless. She also spent time in San Francisco talking and listening to the life stories of people on the street, and gained a new appreciation for their courage and caring. "I saw honesty and integrity among them. The homeless care for each other in their own way and often look out for those who they feel are worse off. It was an eye-opening experience." Melanie feels safe and secure when she is working in homeless shelters and talking with people living on the street, "There is a driving force within me and I'm not always sure where it comes from, but it overpowers any fear I have."

Melanie is currently finding new ways to channel her passion for helping others. She recently set up a food bank that distributes food to women and families throughout her rural community. As she delivers to her clients' homes she is aware of the women in the community experiencing domestic abuse, and she is committed to helping these women escape their confined lives. "I want them to reach outside of where they are and see a bigger picture, and to know that, although they may feel hope is gone, it isn't. I hope my experiences throughout my own life will assist others who may be starting their journey out of their cages."

Celia ✕ Making It Happen

"Courage is the capability to move past one's fears into the unknown with strong conviction as the label of choice."

Celia's life is a a story of moving into the unknown armed with strong conviction. She was born in the Philippines in a Manilla ghetto and her parents struggled to support her and her siblings. Her father had a dream, however, that at least one of their children would escape the poverty the family endured. Even though her parents earned little money, they paid for Celia to go to college and saved enough of their meager earnings for Celia to someday immigrate to the United States.

Celia pushed herself to get the civil engineering diploma she needed to become respected in her trade. Due to the Vietnam War there was a shortage of professional engineers in the United States and the U.S. Department of Labor began recruiting engineers throughout the world. Celia grabbed at the chance to leave the Phillipines. When she was accepted and issued her work visa she was given only two weeks until she had to leave. "The more you think about some things the more scared you get. Sometimes you just have to go. Like swimming, you just go in." That's exactly what she did.

She arrived in New Mexico in 1968 knowing no one and with only $300 to her name. She still had the hope of a job though, along with her dream of success and determination to work as an engineer. Little did Celia know that she would face a long battle of gender discrimination and that she would have to start from scratch in her profession.

Celia quickly discovered that the engineering field was dominated by men and that no one wanted to hire her because she was a woman. She decided right away she couldn't wait around hoping someone else would make it happen. "I came here to work. I was told they needed engineers and so I applied to come to this country and was accepted. But I found out I had to fight to practice my trade and find my space." She drew on the perseverance she had developed throughout a lifetime of overcoming obstacles.

After much difficulty and searching Celia finally landed a job as a surveyor's assistant, and later as a junior designer. "It was shocking because I thought the United States would be more advanced." She found that being accepted as an immigrant woman in her profession was not easy, but she never let that keep her down. "An immigrant female engineer was new to everyone so I had to learn to expect different kinds of reaction. It's just a matter of educating people."

Eventually Celia did educate the people in her profession and she was able to build a very successful career by creating a business she loves. Celia believes "You get into something and it is only because you believe you can do it. You have to know yourself. It all starts there. Know your own strength—know what you know and then you can make decisions based on that. You can make things happen."

Evelyn ✕ Moving with the Ebb and Flow

From the outside it looks like Evelyn has lived a charmed life. She has a fabulous career, a strong marriage, and three great sons. Still, she has learned the hard way that each individual defines success in their own way.

It was never a question whether Evelyn would do well in school, get a college education, or give back to her community. Her father's military background and traditional Catholic upbringing influenced her high expectations of herself. And she made good on those expectations. As a part of the first graduating class to include women, she was captain of the volleyball team and president of the student body of her Catholic high school. Evelyn was a Type A personality, had a strong drive, and was a goal setter.

She began her career with a large CPA firm. Evelyn worked on expanding her responsibilities and roles for seven years when she decided she wanted to start a family. What she saw troubled her. "I looked up the ladder and saw that all of the female partners were divorced or single. There weren't any good role models for the life I wanted." It was then that Evelyn made the first of many courageous decisions to bring her work life into balance, decisions she continues to make today. She left the firm and took a position with a bank, starting over in a new position and as a new mother.

It took a lot of courage for Evelyn to switch firms and adjust her career path to create space in her life for a young family, but it took even more courage to look at herself and see that she continued to exhibit extreme Type A behavior. "I realized I was trying to prove I could do it all—career, wife, mother. I thought I was going to be superwoman, but I started to resent that my one hour of free time was going grocery shopping." That realization changed the course of her career. "I realized if I really wanted to live a much longer life I had to choose where and how I wanted to spend my time and how I reacted to things around me."

Evelyn says her life is about adjusting. She put herself on a crash course of learning to delegate more around the home and office. And then Evelyn did something very surprising. She reconnected with her first love—volleyball. "I began coaching girls volleyball, and then, before I knew it, I was running a program for the grammar school and even coaching boys and girls volleyball." The reconnection with sports was just what she needed to let go of taking herself too seriously.

As her career progressed Evelyn was one step away from becoming the Chief Financial Officer of her firm when she realized she didn't want to work in finance anymore. She found she lacked the enthusiasm for being the last step in the corporate decision-making process. Most people thought she was crazy, but she began looking for opportunities within the firm that would allow her to explore her passion for contributing to the strategic vision. She took a step back into general management and began to connect with a new energy for her career. "In many cases the hardest thing I've had to do is give up on the notion of having a clear mentor and a clear path."

At each level of her career she had to look at a new level of balance, a new way of finding what works for her and her family. When she was hand-picked to become the Chief of Staff to the new CEO, she courageously laid out firm guidelines and boundaries for her position that would allow her to maintain the balance she had worked so hard to develop. The position grew and soon Evelyn found herself taking on responsibilities for a recent merger and commuting from coast to coast one full week a month. Energizing? Yes! Work–life balance? Hardly!

Six months into the role she could see things needed to change. To Evelyn courage is, "being willing to not have such hard-set plans and recognize that you will have to adjust them along the way."

So yet another career shift and another starting over began.

"I think there is an element of courage which allows us to recover from our setbacks. Courage speaks to our reaction to setbacks. How long does it take you to remember you have a choice—a choice to move forward?" Keeping this perspective in mind, Evelyn has been able to see that there is an ebb and flow to her career and a natural rhythm that needs to be honored. "It's been a fun ride, but I think if there is any courageous part in this it's that I stayed willing to move, not knowing for certain where it would lead."

Julie ⚬ Finding Peace in the Midst of Chaos

Even as a young woman Julie believed that giving away your worldly goods and helping other people was the path to true peacefulness. So as a young professional without many resources, Julie gave of herself to make up for what she couldn't give in material possessions. Constantly giving to others she took responsibility for being there, being in control, and fixing it for everyone and everything. As a result she developed the chronic illness called fibromyalgia.

She learned to move beyond her chronic pain with the help of a practioner who encouraged her to incorporate meditation, yoga, exercise, and extreme self-care into her life. She learned that giving, giving, and giving to others without giving to herself was not an answer; she decided she needed greater balance between helping others and helping herself. Thankfully, the physical and emotional lessons she learned allowed her to live symptom-free. But that's not the end of her story.

When Julie accepted a new position as executive director for a women's self-employment initiative, she had no idea of the transformation she was about to lead. Power struggles, unresolved conflicts, and unstated resentments had taken a toll on the board and the effectiveness of the organization. Julie knew that changes in the board membership could mean dramatic shifts in their funding sources, as the person raising the most money was likely be the one to leave, taking her purse with her. On top of their already dwindling resources a major delay in federal government support created a year-long operating crisis.

With a deep breath, Julie took the steps needed to change the power paradigm from money to mission to unlock the organization's true potential. Continuing through that year took the most courage of anything Julie had ever done. "You have no idea how badly I wanted to say, 'You know what, I've got a family, I'm not doing this—I didn't sign up for this.'"

Julie knew from deep within that she was supposed to go through this particular challenge at this time. For her it was a journey of finding peace in the midst of chaos and knowing she was doing the right thing. "I looked inside myself, acknowledged the balance in the life I had created with my partner, my children, and my spirituality. I forced myself to stay connected to the physical practices of yoga and running. When I could I sat and stared at the wall for as long as I could stand it, which is my version of meditation." These were the tools that helped Julie through her illness and now they were supporting her in her challenging work.

As the agency teetered on the edge, Julie knew if she went back to her old ways of being responsible for everyone and trying to control it all so it wouldn't fall apart, she would be putting her own health at risk. She also knew she was responsible for creating something new—at the agency and in her life.

"I had to develop as a leader. I started out thinking everything was going to be by consensus, but you know what, that's not the way it works. At some point, somebody has to lead. Someone has to make the hard decisions. I worked with the staff from a place of honesty. I told them what was going on from a place of authenticity. I didn't try to play games and tell them it was going to be OK, I just presented the reality of the situation. I recall one time I had to tell the staff that I didn't think we'd make the payroll. I gave them all the information and told them they had to make the choice themselves, but that I hoped they would stay. They all did."

For over a year Julie worked at acknowledging the organization was best served when she respected herself first. She learned to trust herself, even when others didn't necessarily agree with her views or her decisions. She learned to trust that she had a perspective as the leader that was worth listening to. She learned that stepping up to the responsibility of being a leader did not mean she had to do it all, see it all, or be it all. As Julie learned to trust her abilities, knowing she was doing the right thing, her staff learned to trust her, too.

Would she call herself courageous? "Yes! I feel like I've earned it! I had to pull something out from the depths of everything I had. So, you know what, I crossed a threshold. I still have great courage, not every moment of every day, but mostly. Everything that I had, I had inside me, just waiting to come out."

Lynn x R-E-S-P-E-C-T

The year was 1967 and Lynn, a young twenty-something school teacher in the northern United States, wore a pair of slacks to work to ward off the harsh winter chill. Her principal called her into his office and told her "With legs like yours, I don't want them covered up. Don't wear slacks again. Do you understand?" Lynn understood all right. Having grown up with a domineering father, she understood plenty. Lynn approached her female colleagues, most of whom were twenty years her senior, described her dilemma and asked for their help. Two days later all the women teachers wore pants to work. The dress code was broken and Lynn was certain she and the principal had a new understanding.

That was many years, many travels, and many courageous moments ago. Together they all add up to one incredible life that sometimes reads like a movie script about the women's movement. "I think I'm a risk-taker who takes time to get good information," says Lynn as she reflects on her life. "I just try to assert myself and do my best, but not be disrespectful." That approach has led her on some very interesting and rewarding journeys.

As a young wife and new mother, Lynn accepted a teaching

assignment that required she pack up her family and move to the tiny island of Yak in Micronesia as a contract teacher with the Department of Interior. Their time living on an island with no phones and just once-a-week visits from the supply plane was an adventure in more ways than one. "As a feminist, it was also very interesting. In a society where women go topless, walk behind the men, and cross the road as a sign of respect my whole attitude had to be—we're not here to change them. I went with the idea that I was there to learn as much as to teach."

That drive and determination to show unrelenting respect for herself and others is what made Lynn a world-class teacher and mentor to literally thousands of young people in her community and in the world. "As a teacher I always tried to encourage young men and women to be all they could be and to make wise choices about their lives." Once, she took the risk of confronting a young female student on her alcohol use. Ultimately, the girl became her foster daughter and lived with Lynn for three years while she completed school. She graduated with a 3.5 GPA, excelled in sports, and today has a successful career as a detective.

Lynn was always ready to learn the lessons she taught. When her twenty-five year marriage ended, Lynn promised herself that she would not go out on a date or get into any relationship for two years. "I got married when I was twenty years old and a senior in college. I needed to know if I could live alone and I needed to know if I could support myself. I found out the answers were 'yes.' I decided that if I was going to let somebody in my life it would be my choice. It would not be because I was needy or I couldn't earn my own money or I needed someone to take care of me. So now the person I am with is someone I want to be with; he is very good to me and respects me."

But respect for others can sometimes be difficult. One of the most painful decisions Lynn has ever had to make was respecting her mother's end-of-life wishes. For several years, her mother's health had been deteriorating, and less than a year after Lynn's father died her mother was hospitalized with little hope of recovery. The doctor took Lynn aside and reminded her that her mother's Living Will stated her mother asked for no extraordinary means. "I kept thinking, I don't know what to do, I don't know what to do. Finally I accepted that this is what my mother wanted. I just sat and held her hand. It was so hard. I knew when she died I would be all alone, but I had to do what she wanted. It still bothers me. It's been ten years and I think it was the hardest thing I've ever done." Even harder it seems than facing her own mortality.

Lynn has been diagnosed with cancer three times and each

time she faced it with determination, humor, and compassion for herself. The night before her mastectomy Lynn had a conversation with her breasts and said, "You know, we've been really good pals, I really enjoyed you a lot, but I'm not my breasts. So...see you around." Her surgeon was adamant that her reconstructed breast look realistic, complete with a tattooed areola, but Lynn didn't necessarily see the value. "I told him, 'The people in my life don't care, I don't care, and all the doctors and nurses who have seen me naked were once my students, so I'm over being modest. But if it makes you happy to tattoo on an areola, we're going to be partners in this and I'm going to have a say in it. If you insist on doing this I'm having the feminist symbol as the tattoo.' He looked at me in disbelief and said, 'Are you kidding?' I simply responded, 'I would never kid about something like that.'"

It's Ours ⚹ Share It

It's Ours x Share It

You are not here merely to make a living. You are here in order to enable the world to live more amply, with greater vision, with a finer spirit of hope and achievement. You are here to enrich the world and you impoverish yourself if you forget the errand.

—W. WILSON

THE WORLD DESPERATELY needs women. It needs our wisdom and intuition, creativity, bridge-building skills, and our ability to cut to the heart of a matter. The world needs our long-term thinking and our capacity to take action with clear understanding of the impact it will have on the health of the globe. The world needs our willingness to share—our ideas, encouragement, power, and courage.

Sometimes, it seems hopeless. On the surface all we see is chaos and confusion—in essence, a breakdown of all our traditions and systems. Is there any portion of society and the world that doesn't seem to be falling apart? Is there any doubt that each of us feels perplexed and frustrated with the direction the world is headed and our ability to impact and change it?

Like an iceberg, however, there is much hidden below the

surface. A growing current of positive change is flowing steadily and quietly under the surface. A significant transformation is going on. Women are asking difficult questions, women are challenging old and ineffective systems, and women are leading us toward new types of relationships and thinking. Women, everywhere, are positively changing the world in large and small ways.

With an emphasis on long-term solutions, shared understanding, collaboration, and action combined with reflection, women are changing the fundamental nature of organizations, political structures, workplaces and families. Together, in partnership with evolved men, new frameworks for social change are being developed. So, while it may sometimes look like the world is falling apart, there is great hope!

WOMEN ARE THE HOPE

Women's role in the world as social change agents and peacemakers is well supported in study after study. The 2004 United Nations white paper titled, "10 Stories the World Should Hear More About," explains:

> While too often reporting of women in conflict situations shows them as powerless victims, the reality,

often glossed over, is that in post-conflict situations women are in the forefront when it comes to negotiating and building peace. Women, who know the price of conflict so well, are also better equipped than men to prevent or resolve it. For generations, women have served as peace educators, both in their families and in their societies. They have proved instrumental in building bridges rather than walls.

When we, as women, advocate and bring about change it benefits not only our self and other women, but men as well. When a woman, for example, guided by her desire for greater balance between work and parenting, requests a more flexible work schedule, this change also benefits the men in the company who want greater balance in their lives. The ripple effect of a woman's act of self-determination, power, and courage emanates outward, changing the world in many ways for many people. Women are in a much better position to bring about many of the needed changes because we have much less to lose. We have been under the radar for so long and far less involved in creating the current systems and so are not as invested in them. Instigating change becomes much more threatening to a man's position, status, and standing in the community if he is advocating a shake-up of the dominant structure and system; a structure and system he is a part of in so many ways. Many men are as frustrated as women with the manner in which problems and issues are being addressed, and in the structures that do not support individuals, families, or communities. Women *changing the world* benefits us all.

A greater recognition and acknowledgement of the many positive changes and women's roles in creating them is needed. The undercurrents of a transformation coming from women's everyday efforts are often not seen or appreciated either by those looking from the outside in or even by women working from the inside.

In much the same way as we have done with self-determination, power, and courage, women have accepted the traditional or old Code. Women have been laboring under old definitions and, as a result, we have diminished ourselves and our efforts. We have not seen ourselves as creating social change because the world often uses a male-oriented definition. We need a new Code for *changing the world.* A Code that reflects and honors the multitude of ways in which women are having an impact.

THE OLD CODE

When most of us hear the words, "changing the world," we go into overwhelm. As mere mortals already struggling with the everyday challenges that threaten to drown us at times, how can we change, really *change* the world? Using the old Code we automatically think of grand scale efforts at the hands of selfless individuals who dedicate their lives to a single cause or purpose. From the stories we hear and the books we read it is clear that this dedication to their singular mission demands great sacrifice and penetrating focus over years. Our image is of individuals fueled by a burning passion that ignites their decisions to pack up and leave secure jobs to walk thousands of miles, give up all worldly goods, or move in with a nomadic African tribe. Think Mother Teresa, Joan of Arc, and Peace Pilgrim. Their stories are awe-inspiring. Their contributions and courage serve as a beacon for hope, and their examples motivate us to examine and strengthen our own altruism and willingness to serve others.

Our society's social-change heroines and heroes have made tremendous contributions and they are deserving of our admiration and awe. Unfortunately, they serve as our *only* role models for *people who change the world* and have become the template by which we measure ourselves. We put them on a pedestal; we make them the ideal to follow if we want to make a difference.

Too often, however, our awe is also accompanied by a sense of disappointment in ourselves. Women look to these role models and think diminishing thoughts such as *What a slacker I am…I am not changing the world in any way!* Because we believe anything less than quitting our job or leaving our family to pack up and volunteer in some distant land, can't be considered as *changing the world.*

We do not understand that behind the perfect role model images are living, breathing human beings with trials and tribulations just like the rest of us. We usually do not see or know the winding trail their lives have taken—the ups and downs—as they climb their way towards their dedicated choice. In comparison our efforts do not seem to be grand scale, we are not entirely selfless, we do not want to make the sacrifice to leave our job or family, and our focus is hardly single-minded. Women are quick to believe that, next to Mother Teresa, their lives have little purpose or meaning. We assume our everyday efforts are making little difference.

The truth is, women's daily efforts are simply not acknowledged, much less honored, by society. As a result, women do not appreciate or honor their own efforts. We have bought our culture's conventional Code for those who change the world. We do not even equate "making a difference" or "having an impact" with *changing the world.*

The women we interviewed were uncomfortable with the idea that they were changing the world, though they did see they were *impacting* the world in many different ways. They understood their words and deeds had impact in their families, workplace, and community. What they did not fully understand was how that impact *changes* the world. This we believe is tied to the sheer grandiosity of the concept. They could wrap their minds around the idea of impacting the world, not changing the world. A slight difference in wording equals a huge difference in perception. Redefining the Code gives women's contributions greater fanfare by bringing the concept down to human scale and allowing us to understand and acknowledge the significance of our efforts.

In actuality, we change the world in all we do. Our words and actions do have a ripple effect, seen or unseen. At times we can immediately see or feel the impact, as in some change we might introduce, or a conversation we have. Other times we do not have a clue whether our act of kindness or courage in tackling a tough issue made a difference at all. Nonetheless, we impact others and situations either positively or negatively in everything we do and those effects ripple outward.

The bad news is that it can seem daunting and disappointing to think we cannot just skate through life, doing our own thing, and not worrying about how we affect others and the world. The good news is that we can begin to understand how significant our life is and how much impact we really can and do have.

This understanding is important. When we diminish our value and begin to think we are *less than,* we deny the gifts we were brought into the world to use. We keep them hidden and small because we get the message that the world considers them to be small.

When we do not feel we have value or our efforts have value, a nasty cycle begins. We make a decision, unconsciously, to be something other than we are; usually, it turns out to be something not as creative or energetic or powerful as we were really meant to be. We tuck away some or many of our authentic parts and so diminish who we truly are and how we were meant to serve the world. When we do not bring our gifts—talents, insights, and power fully into the world or allow others to do the same, everyone loses out. Disempowerment is a gift that keeps on giving.

When we think of changing the world we do not necessarily think about women, who, day in and day out, are making a difference. Rarely do we hear about women who are changing the world by shifting a conversation they are involved in so that it results in greater understanding and collaboration, or by raising strong, respectful, self-determined children. We do not put women on a pedestal for pursuing a craft or raising a difficult issue as means of expressing themselves fully, and thus, inspiring people around them to do the same. Yet, every woman makes a difference.

HISTORIC CONVERGENCE

Never before have women been such a force. Due to the convergence of four factors, this is a unique point in history putting women in the strongest position ever to transform the world for the better.

1. Women have enormous financial clout.

There have never been greater numbers of women with ever-increasing financial resources. While there still remains a significant gap between women's and men's earnings, our financial clout is huge. In the U.S. women make the majority of purchasing decisions on products and services. We make decisions about the types of health care, nutrition, and clothing our family needs and gets, the types of cars that are driven, and the recreational activities that are pursued. Women literally hold the purse strings.

Younger women have greater access to job opportunities that pay well, and as a result, have more discretionary income than ever before. Many mid-life women have worked for years and have accumulated greater wealth, or are financially comfortable through spousal retirement, inheritance and other means. Of the U.S. households with an income of more than $600,000, 40% are headed by women. Our growing financial power is formidable.

All age groups of women, because we are used to making the vast majority of consumer decisions for our families, are skilled in managing finances. As new avenues have expanded to educate women about investment and money management strategies, we are becoming very savvy personal finance managers. More and more of us are taking an active role in determining the course of our financial future and realizing we have the power to put our money where our mouth is. We are able to funnel money into causes we care about.

The recent focus on women's philanthropy through women-only giving circles also provides women with ever-greater control and impact on the distribution of our country's finances. The most popular issues these giving circles support are youth development, women and girls' empowerment, human services, and mental health/crisis intervention. This supports Eleanor Roosevelt's observation in her 1933 book, *It's Up to the Women,* "Only women in power would consider the needs of women without power."

2. Women have confidence and moxie.

Today's younger women grew up with strong messages about the importance of living more independent lives; families, schools, and communities have done much to strengthen their self-sufficiency. More women than ever are enrolled in college, providing us with education, skills, and confidence for making our own way. Since the 1972 introduction of Title IX, a federal law prohibiting sex discrimination in athletics, the number of girls participating in sports has exploded. In addition to our involvement in sports, we have opportunities to watch other high school, collegiate, and professional female athletes in every sport challenge all limits. This has given girls and younger women confidence about participating and performing in the world of athletics and in all areas of their lives. In general, younger women are more comfortable with their own strength, power and courage, and believe they have the right to live a life of their own choosing.

Women, aged 45–65, often grew up with activist ideals and a history of questioning traditional systems and beliefs. Now in mid-life we are adding a heavy dose of assertiveness, strength, confidence, wisdom, and feistiness to the mix. We have arrived at a point in our lives where we appreciate the depth and value of our experience and knowledge and are no longer satisfied with taking a back seat.

Women of every age are pushing back in society, demanding acceptance, inclusion, and equality. Thankfully, some new policies and legislation have been introduced and passed, including the Family Leave Act, domestic partner benefits, and higher standards for child-care providers.

3. Women expect environments responsive to their needs.

Many women combine parenting with career, and creating greater work/life balance is a goal for women of all ages. We want and need employers to be more flexible with work hours, job responsibilities, etc., and we are forcing organizations and businesses to change. If progress isn't seen, women are likely to seek other, more responsive work environments. We may find another employer who will accommodate our needs, set out to create an entrepreneurial opportunity for ourselves, or opt out from the work world altogether. Opting out defines the rising trend toward women leaving corporate positions for alternative career paths. Women, by opting out permanently or temporarily, are sending a clear message about their needs for balance, and forcing corporations to explore innovative programs to retain talented women.

Mid-life women have reached a place in their lives where they are quick to recognize, but not accept, disempowering unhealthy environments. They also have less patience for status quo in general, and are comfortable challenging traditional, often male-dominated, systems. The new term to identify this age group, "Fuck You 50s" (coined by Suzanne Braun Levine in *Inventing the Rest of Our Lives: Women in Second Adulthood)*, came about for good reasons.

As our women interviewees so often told us, finding meaning, not just financial security or status, has become their goal. As a result, they are more discerning in their choices; less willing to accept situations that don't allow them to do meaningful work or have meaningful relationships.

After many years of facing limited personal and professional opportunities, there is an exodus of women leaving mainstream employment for entrepreneurial endeavors. Women are the main contributors to the recent explosion of new small businesses. Many of our women interviewees started businesses to gain greater autonomy, flexibility, and decision-making authority. As entrepreneurs we are tapping into a new level of creativity and self-determination that is significantly impacting the fabric and economy of our country.

4. Women know how to make a positive difference.

Women around the world are united in their desire to make a difference. Giving to others and serving the world in large and small ways has become second nature. Because the majority of us have been raised to be caregivers, we are geared to thinking about our lives in terms of how much we are giving to others. We often measure our value by how well we are serving and caring for other people.

Women bring unique skills and abilities to care giving. Women have the special ability to see through what is transient to what is truly important, and we tend to be the keepers of the values for our families and for society. Study after study has found that women are most often the voice advocating for changes related to broad societal issues including environment, peace and justice, poverty, domestic abuse, child abuse, education, and housing. According to Sally Helgesen, author of *The Female Advantage,* one of the characteristics that distinguishes women's leadership is how they see their work as "encompassing a vision of society—they relate decisions to the larger effect on the role of the family, the American educational system, the environment, even world peace. They feel they must make a difference in the world."

Given this convergence of powerful factors, women are a force to be reckoned with. We are at a point in history where we hold the future in our hands. Women are needed—our voices, our wisdom, our ability to build relationships, and our resiliency— to effectively solve the enormous problems the world is facing. As Marie Wilson, founder of The White House Project says, "When we stop to think about the leadership qualities we truly need in the world, the conclusion is starkly obvious: Send in some women!"

A NEW CODE

The old Code is based on the notion that we only change the world through bold, heroic, self-sacrificing actions. The new Code:

• Supports each individual's contribution, and understands that every action an individual takes and every decision an individual makes has an impact on the vitality of our environment, families, community, and world.

• Respects the unique way each of us is making a difference in the world—some by listening and creating a safe, accepting space that supports our growth, some through scaling a mountain and inspiring us to push our own limits.

• Recognizes that we change the world simply by being who we authentically are. When we live in such a way that expresses who we truly are we create a ripple effect, shaping and changing all in our path, in ways we often do not even know.

SHARING THE NEW CODE

The ways women change the world, everyday, in large and small ways is endless and would take years to list them all. However, there are four key ways we transform our world.

1. Living Our Life Fully

We change the world by bringing our gifts and talents fully into the world. When women express themselves honestly and authentically it's a beautiful thing. Every dimension of our life is enriched—our relationships, creativity, physical health, work, spiritual vitality, and financial abundance. When we express ourselves through a craft we are inspired about, have an honest conversation about a difficult issue, do paid or volunteer work that makes our heart glad, or find our own spiritual path, we enhance the world. Author, speaker and spiritual teacher, Marianne Williamson says, "As we let our own light shine, we unconsciously give other people permission to do the same. As we are liberated from our fear, our presence automatically liberates others."

When we live authentically we serve as role models to those who also wish to live authentically. By being comfortable living in our own skin we show others how to feel good living in theirs. The women we interviewed are a testament to living lives fully so as to experience joy and satisfaction—feelings that are contagious and inspiring to others. These women, like so many others, demonstrate how we change the world by simply following our heart, our true north. Whether they are living fully by working in meaningful jobs, raising children, playing music, writing poetry, creating and upholding laws, or participating in sports, these women are serving the world in their own unique way. We live fully not only to enrich our own lives, but also to enrich the lives of others. When we do, we change the world.

2. Changing the Conversation

The foundation of all human systems—whether we're talking about societies, workplaces, families, or couples—is relationships. Relationships are formed around the interactions and conversations we have. If we want to create big changes, we change the little conversations.

There are lots of ways to change the conversation and often the results are amazing. We can raise an uncomfortable topic we have avoided in the past, we can choose to listen and try to understand the other person's viewpoint rather than becoming immediately defensive, or we can express our need instead of acquiescing to someone else's. We cannot change people—we can only change ourselves. And by changing the conversation we can change the pattern of interaction. The woman who speaks up for herself after a long history of being silent changes the pattern and thus, the relationship, in that moment. Maybe it happens ever so subtly, perhaps even invisibly, but when the words leave her mouth a powerful message is communicated to others about who she is and how she wants to be treated.

The message she sends in that moment is not only received by the person she is speaking to, but also by herself, *I really did have the courage to say what I thought. I really am a courageous woman! It really doesn't matter if anything changes, it was still important for me to say what I wanted.* This momentary feeling can fuel additional acts of self-determination, power and courage. As our women interviewees described, when they learned to see themselves differently it changed all their relationships and interactions ultimately for the good. Sometimes the changes were positive and created deeper, more meaningful relationships. Other changes were initially more difficult and seemingly negative, but in the end resulted in each woman tapping into a deeper well of self-determination, power, and courage.

Changing the conversation is a very powerful tool for bringing about change on a larger scale. Consider what might happen if our political and business leaders shifted the conversations with other global leaders from how to create war to how to create peace, or from reducing poverty to eliminating it entirely. What would happen if the conversation shifted to how to include women, as full partners, in solving the global problems of today? Changing the conversation changes the world.

3. Raising Compassionate, Self-Determined Children

The importance of our role as adults and parents in shaping children's perceptions of themselves and others cannot be underestimated. Over and over again, our women interviewees spoke about how strongly they were influenced by what they saw and heard from their mothers, fathers, and other adults in their life. It did not matter if we were talking about power, courage, self-determination, or changing the world, they all felt that encouragement and support, or the lack of it, was a significant factor in their lives. From the examples their parents set, especially the mothers, women learned about assertiveness, diversity, and expressing themselves in the world.

Through positive messages and healthy role modeling as mothers, aunts, teachers, and leaders, the women we spoke with were equipping children with skills and confidence to express their own gifts more fully and to better serve the world. They described the ways in which they consciously and with clear intention exposed their children to different viewpoints and lifestyles, reinforcing the beauty of diversity. They asked for input from the kids, showing them their opinions and ideas mattered. They encouraged the children to follow their hearts, in making educational, career and life choices, supporting fulfillment and joy as worthy goals.

Most importantly, they modeled the value and importance of creating a life based on what they felt was right for them. By the choices they were making these women were a living example to their families. While they were very cognizant of the impact of their decisions and choices on their children and families, they demonstrated they were the final arbiter for their life. By creating a life filled with purpose and meaning, they demon strated power, courage, and self-determination for their children. As Gail McMeekin says in *The 12 Secrets of Highly Creative Women,* "Modeling martyrdom does not teach our daughters how to be happy, authentic women." For many of the women with older children who have left home and established their own lives, the deep sense of purpose and passion their children now have is evident. They were pleased to note that their children were now living happy, healthy lives, and contributing to the betterment of the world in their own special way.

4. Supporting and Encouraging Other Women

Women are often very rough on other women. Another woman accomplishes something and we make denigrating comments about them behind their backs. She works outside the house and we put her down for it. She decides to stay home to raise her children and we judge her harshly. We do not vote for women candidates because we are not used to seeing a woman in a power role. There are a million different ways women do not support other women in their decisions, life choices, and means of self-expression. And yet, undermining another woman simply serves to undermine the power, courage, and self-determination of all women. As Joan L. Bolker, in her essay "A Room of One's Own Is Not Enough" from the book *The Writer's Home*

Companion, says, "The divide-and-conquer dynamic among women keeps too many women guilty, silent, and unexpressed. The whole point of the women's movement has been freedom of choice—a society that grants every woman the freedom to choose what's best of her as a unique individual."

The women we interviewed talked about the shift they made in their lives to truly accepting and supporting other women's accomplishments. They realized that this change came about as they began to like and accept *themselves* better. Many women gave examples of dramatic differences in their lives when they realized the subtle, but significant ways they undermined other women; the times they made a snide comment under their breath about a woman's way of dressing, or the competition they created when a woman received some public recognition for an accomplishment. As they strengthened their own self esteem they were able to stop comparing themselves to other women, and let go of their need to diminish other women's self-expressions.

When another woman accomplishes something she feels is important, rather than choosing to feel threatened by her accomplishment, we can celebrate and honor her. When a woman makes a choice different than we would, we can still appreciate the choice and applaud the self-expression it represents. We can encourage and mentor other women in building skills and experience. "Everyone knows at least one woman who should be urged to follow her dream, a woman who is utterly capable of being more than she is if only she were given encouragement. We need to find her and feed her ambition. Don't wait for the culture to change. Change it yourself by helping others to step forward," says Marie Wilson in *Closing the Leadership Gap.*

We can encourage and support women as they achieve political positions. According to the Women's Environment and Development Organization, "The number of women members of government has risen less than 3 percentage points since the Fourth World Conference on Women in Beijing in 1995. At that rate, it will take 75 years before women have equal representation in their national governments." Although women comprise 51% of the U.S. population, the numbers of women holding political leadership positions is dismal. If we ever hope to achieve some level of parity, we must support women whose values we trust and help them succeed.

We are all in this together. If we want to capitalize on the force that women are for change in the world, we need to support each other in all our varied means of self-expression. Wilson says, "If we hold one another back instead of pushing one another forward, we will most certainly stay stuck." It will take all of us together, sharing knowledge, wisdom and encouragement, to change the world.

STORIES OF SHARING IT

Here are stories from women who are changing the world by sharing their self-determination, power, and courage with others. Each woman, in her own way, is living her deep commitment to the feminine principles of intuition, inclusion, bridge-building, and collaboration. These women are the voices of conscience and wisdom, and the hands that are raised in challenging the old Codes. Their stories highlight how each of us, in everyday ways, is a force for positive changes in the world.

Mary X Believing in Miracles

"I knew going in that somebody was going to have to face the music. I knew that it was going to be me. It was as much a part of my work as the good part. It was as much my role to see this through the darkness as it was through the glory."

It's never easy when doors close on your dreams. And it's even more frustrating when it's the culmination of your life's work. For Mary, her dream is creating a comprehensive residential treatment program and center for addicted mothers and their children so they can remain a family while pulling together the pieces of a life not driven by addiction. Mary brought all her wisdom, skill, and energy to this landmark program for women that worked in favor of the family. Of course, it never occurred to her it would not succeed. Even though the facility closed its doors after two and a half years of operation, it was anything but a failure.

Mary says she has always seen the courageous side of women. At age seventeen she entered the community of the Sisters of St. Joseph's, leaving behind friends and family to take vows of poverty, chastity, and obedience. "I was completely immersed in a woman's world. Women ran the business, women built the building, women made the decisions. Because I was so young, I internalized that this is absolutely what women could do."

After seven years of teaching elementary students from the privileged neighborhood supported by the convent, Mary was restless and eager to make a greater contribution in the world. When she was turned down for mission work in Bolivia, she made the difficult decision to leave the order and strike out on her own. Mary accepted a teaching position in an urban community that was struggling with racial issues, poverty, and drugs. Many of the children were labeled at-risk. She was now face-to-face with real needs and was beginning to sense her real mission in life. As her career in the school system developed, Mary began working with younger children until she eventually was assigned to pre-schoolers. It required that she make home visits to talk with the mostly single mothers about their child's development. "I saw a lot of addicted mothers—women with no support system, no car, no phone, no one to turn to, who were living in fear. And they were unfortunately teaching their children to manage their fear and their lives with alcohol or drugs. Addiction kills the will—it's so damaging, so shaming. There is not a population in the country more ashamed than addicted mothers of small children."

Mary knows that from personal experience. "Most people think the curious part of my story is that I am an ex-nun. I think the most interesting part, the part that caused me the most shame and the most transformation, is that I am an alcoholic woman."

When Mary left the convent at twenty-five she moved back home to live with her parents. Both professionals, her mother and father would drink every evening at the close of their work day and continue through dinner and into the night. Mary could see that their drinking of hard liquor was a growing issue and was determined not to repeat the pattern. So, naïvely, she chose to drink wine instead. Soon Mary found herself consuming several glasses each evening and her addiction was well underway.

As her life went on, she married and had four children. Mary managed to stay high-functioning while holding down a job, volunteering in the community, and playing the roles of wife and mother. But the drinking did not let up and Mary realized she needed help. "I was so ashamed. I took the phone into the closet to make the call to the treatment program even though no one was at home. I waited until my mother and sister were out of the country because I knew they would try to talk me out of exposing our family to the shame. I was a lucky woman. I never lost a job, my wonderful husband supported me, and even my family helped. And even then, in the middle of all of it my deepest fear was that somebody could take my children because of my addiction. I knew I had a problem for probably five years, but I kept it a secret because I was convinced I would lose my children. So if it was that paralyzing for me, a privileged woman in a supportive marriage, I could just imagine a single mother or a woman with an abusive husband feeling like there were absolutely no options."

So Mary's journey of recovery started her on the road to helping other mothers with theirs. Ultimately, it led her to the creation of a family residential treatment center with comprehensive services for mothers and their children. Mary, along with a group of people committed to her vision, renovated an historic house that was close to being condemned and turned it into a beautiful, comforting home. Mary says, "It was a miracle to watch this old building come to life, like a phoenix rising from the ashes. I felt like I was watching a miracle unfolding." From the moment they opened the doors they operated at capacity.

By keeping the families together, the program supported the women in triumphing over addiction and best of all, modeling recovery for their children. The cycle of shame and defeat could be broken and the next generation would know there are options. Mary believes there is no one more courageous than the women who walk up the steps to the center carrying their children. "I would define courage as what we do in our dark moments. How you hang onto your spirit when all indications are that you have failed. I tell women—you have no idea the degree to which you have exhibited your power today—now you can move from this place, now you can change your world."

The ground-breaking treatment center was fraught with difficulty and controversy. As a nonprofit organization, they relied on funding from many outside sources. Traditional funding agencies didn't know how to categorize the program and so money earmarked for treatment of women's addictions was slow in coming. Several times, Mary made the journey to her state capital to explain the program and its benefits to gain the support of high-ranking officials. And, although the governor was supportive, the state was short of funds itself. The local community did what it could to support the center, but other agencies and programs felt threatened by this change in the treatment paradigm and were not always supportive. So despite all the success in serving these families, the facility closed. Some say it failed.

"It's my belief that if you pay attention, follow the cues that you get from your heart, and do the work in a spirit-filled way, you cannot fail. Even if it looks like you did—you didn't. Nothing is ever going to change if somebody doesn't take a bullet once in awhile. I know I am doing this work out of my own experience. It's my mission, my job. I don't care if it's hard. I don't care if it doesn't go right. I don't have a choice. It's what I must do."

Ubaka ✕ The Drum Song of All Women

"Remember, you come from a long line of strong women."

When you meet Ubaka you immediately understand her sense of power runs deep. So it's not really surprising that she lives by this mantra and consciously gifts it to others.

Unfortunately, Ubaka's childhood was not that different from a lot of girls in her Jersey City neighborhood. As a young girl she was molested, abused, separated from her family, and placed in a foster home for many of her early years.

Even though she received little physical or emotional support from her family, she managed to hold onto her dream. "As a little girl people would ask me what I wanted to be when I grew up. My answer was always 'an art teacher.'" Today Ubaka is an artist, a poet, a musician, and definitely a teacher. She facilitates drumming circles and workshops for women to rediscover their power. "My work here is about liberation and freedom—freedom to be our authentic selves and freedom to become who we are authentically as women."

For Ubaka, the rhythm and calm of the drum is an instant reminder of our first experience—the biological experience of our pulsating blood, the rhythm of our heartbeat, and being born a woman. "As a human, that's the way we get here—through a woman. Now that's powerful. That's what women need to remember."

Although the first part of her life was fraught with fear and isolation, Ubaka credits women in her life with coming along at the right moments to support her and show her the way. "My fourth grade teacher was very religious. She took me to a Catholic church and that catalyzed my relationship with Mary. It began to give me a sense that I could recover, heal the overwhelming pain and suffering from my early years."

When she became a teenager, another teacher and mentor opened a door for Ubaka's healing. The woman introduced her to astrology and for the first time Ubaka began to see that "my life situation was not just controlled by my family or by the social, political structure that supported racism and segregation, but that I did have power and influence over my life and that I could make choices. I could decide."

As she became active in the Civil Rights Movement, Ubaka recognized she did not have to feel directed by her personal history or the political situation. Instead, she could be a part of a process and a movement that could change things. It was then that a third woman came into her life to support her—the abolitionist Harriett Tubman.

One day, that passionate woman from Civil War days who chose not to accept the oppression of slaves, simply stepped into Ubaka's life. "I did not seek her out, but somehow she came into my presence as an example of someone living as such a pioneer. She trusted her own mind and sense about freedom and moved from that place. I feel often that I stand directly on her shoulders, that she holds my ankles. Anytime I feel a little wobbly in the knees I feel that she just tightens her grip and reminds me who I am."

Ubaka feels she receives validation that she's on the right path through the response to her workshops, concerts, and teachings. To stay in this powerful place of courage she "rides the current of other women who have all demonstrated it for me." And she reminds all the women she meets: "Remember, you come from a long line of strong women. And each of us stands in the front of the line."

Mary Ellen ✕ Quiet Courage

"Self-determination is being able to draw on my experience, to recognize things about myself, and to be able to say, I like doing this, I don't like doing that. Then I can start to determine and choose what new experiences I want to investigate and pursue."

At first glance Mary Ellen is a study in contrasts. In one of her professional roles her success depends on her ability to remain absolutely neutral, to be dispassionate. In her other role she is called upon to display passion and, sometimes, indignation. She admits she dislikes confrontation, but everyday she is involved in mediating conflict. She was raised in a typical suburban Midwest neighborhood, yet feels a deep sense of connection with women living in African huts, Calcutta slums, or Afghanistan's desert.

It doesn't take a lot of searching to discover what connects these seemingly disparate qualities. Mary Ellen says she is guided by a commitment to advocating for justice and human dignity, whether she is in a courtroom or working in a community. She brings this passion to the many roles she plays—a leader in the legal field, the executive of an international women's organization, and a volunteer tutor. In doing so, she has come to understand the quieter face of courage.

In all parts of her professional life Mary Ellen is aware that her actions, advice, and decisions impact many people's lives. Her legal work requires her to act courageously, to make decisions that may be met with hostility and anger, to take action unpopular with others, and to stand up to bullies. "There's always the risk that somebody will be unhappy with what I decide. I've just gotten used to that. I think an element of courage is acknowledging there is some sort of danger that I or someone else may be in as a result of my action. Courage is considering the risks and still going ahead."

She deals with conflict daily, but says, "I am not a very confrontational person. In fact, I dislike confrontation very much, which is peculiar given my job." She forges ahead even though it does not always come easy to her, "I think courage is facing what you should. It's recognizing my responsibility and obligations, and carrying them out. Sometimes in dealing with confrontation it's getting to the point where *not* dealing with it is more uncomfortable than dealing with it. Other times, it is recognizing that I have been in this type of situation before and survived it and there is no reason it won't work out again."

Mary Ellen feels a connection with those she encounters in her courtroom, "No matter where we are I think we need to recognize each other as humans." Her deep respect for others allows her to appreciate the impact of her decisions and actions, and supports her in creating a different kind of environment in her courtroom; a more civil place.

As a result of her sense of interconnectedness between all humanity, Mary Ellen has taken on a significant leadership role in an international women's organization dedicated to improving the status of women. Here she can put into action her deep belief that women's rights are human rights. "This is a fundamental human rights issue. It is not just a question of giving women rights; the issue is recognizing that women are already endowed with rights."

Her commitment to social justice issues was sparked when she traveled through Europe in 1967. She didn't know much about the difficulties faced by women in other countries until she met a woman in Tehran who helped her understand fundamentalism and its dangerous impact. That meeting fueled her passion to work towards lifting the status of women. Many years later she was invited to a presentation sponsored by the women's organization she now leads. From that moment on she was hooked, "I found the women members of the group to be fascinating." She has been an active member for 23 years.

Mary Ellen's leadership puts her in front of many audiences, educating them about the needs of women across the globe. "I think women particularly in a developed world need to educate themselves more about the less-developed world and the circumstances in which women live. We all need to figure out how to assist women in reaching their full potential." She sees courage in women's stories of dealing with inequities in pay and rights, lack of resources, and cultural and family attitudes that don't support women. She is committed to helping women create lives of dignity and possibility.

Her understanding of the challenges women throughout the world face help her to always remember how fortunate she has been in her own life, "I think there are some things in your life you get to determine, but a lot of others are just luck of the draw. I would not have this life, presumably, had I been born in a great many parts of the world. I am very lucky."

Pami ✕ Walking with Heart

What would you call a red-headed Jewish mother of twins who wears her spirituality on her sleeve while operating a scrap-booking business and a walking labyrinth? You'd call her Pami. You wouldn't call her Pam, not without being corrected. She feels it's been a long and incredible journey to live into her full "Paminess."

Like many women, Pami began her self-discovery in college. During the beginning of one class, she told the prof and her peers to call her Pam, just Pam. Pam it was. The next semester, the same professor asked her in front of the entire class, "It says your name is Pami, what's this about Pam?" She couldn't answer, she just had to chew on it awhile. What she came to understand was that in denying her true name, she was denying who she really was: Pami.

That true woman is anything but average. When you talk with Pami, you're struck by her connection with the beauty of the natural world. She speaks in the metaphoric language of the mystics with references to what the chickadee or possum had said to her that morning, and yet you sense her feet are planted firmly on the ground.

Pami grew up in a small town in the rural Midwest. She described it as very "white-bread." There were few people of color, and most everyone was Catholic so religious diversity was also scarce. "My college years were about finding out if I held the same fears that prevailed in my community. I consciously opened myself to exploring everything and everyone as a way of expanding my view of the world." Not all her choices were positive or self-affirming; Pami admits many of her behaviors were self-sabotaging and self-destructive. She believes that living through them and their consequences helped her to build a sense of responsibility and to evolve. "I often ask myself, *What must I learn from this?* I've had to learn to let go and move on, like putting up little road markers acknowledging where I've been and then saying good bye."

The journey has taken her to an unexpected spirit-filled life. Pami works with women through scrapbooking. So they learn to take time for themselves and connect with their spirit. "I know absolutely that this is the work I am to do—gathering women and providing a sacred space in which to connect, and yet I have had to work through my own fears of this responsibility."

That's why the labyrinth is so important to Pami and her clients. In the midst of a large walking labyrinth she connects with nature to gain the guidance and perspective to help others.

And when you're the mother of twin six-year-old boys sometimes a little walk in the woods does everyone some good.

Amidst the leaves, trees, chattering birds, and scurrying critters, Pami has come to see herself as a woman of courage and power. "Courage has been a part of my whole adult life, but I have not ever wanted to acknowledge that I was a courageous person because it seems to carry a lot of responsibility somehow. I have been conscious that I have an impact and I feel I am ready to step up and accept what has been divinely given. I feel we receive information all the time, but it takes courage to accept it and act upon that wisdom. That's where I'm at, taking the leaps of faith."

Pami talks easily about the courage other women display in the scrapbooking gatherings. "They all open up and talk about everything in their lives and conclude by making a commitment to take two hours a month to do this work. I always hear the typical resistance—no babysitter, an already full schedule, no support from a spouse, but what they are really saying is they don't feel they deserve to have a life. I hear it over and over from women executives to women who choose to stay at home—they're saying *I don't deserve.* And yet, they reach in and find a way to make their lives a priority and show up the next month."

Pami is aware of the small acts of courage in her life: the

courage to reach out to a stranger on the ski lift, the courage to raise her children in the Jewish faith in a small town, and even the courage to put a bumper sticker on her car during the last presidential election. They seem like little gestures, but they add up to one authentic Pami.

Flora ⚭ Respecting the Power of Others

"It really is true that the strength of the society is the strength of the women."

Flora is a spirited physician who sees beauty in women's strength and power. In her medical practice her vision has been to help women understand and act on their power to create a life of their own choosing. "Women have power through bearing children, through raising children, through not having children, and through not raising children. There is power in all of those, and it's different for every woman." Her goal is for each woman to ask the fundamental questions: *Whose life is this anyway? Who am I doing this for?*

Flora has asked those same questions as she recently reconsidered her life path. "I think I would describe my life as trying to find a new direction because of changes I didn't entirely expect." Her vision was one of building a strong medical practice, focused primarily on women and families. Flora and her business partner worked well together and were pleased with the direction they were moving. However, for health reasons her partner needed to make some changes, causing Flora to begin questioning how satisfied she was with her practice and working in health care in general. She sorted through difficult decisions, *Can I keep my vision? How much do I sacrifice or compromise? What am I unwilling to live with? What is sacred to me? What change do I want to influence in the world?*

It was Flora's desire to impact change that led her in the first place to apply to medical school when she was in her early forties. It was difficult being one of the oldest students, but her vision for expanding how women viewed themselves and their lives sustained her. She was also motivated by the simple desire to survive the rigorous program. "Mainly, as someone who was older and going through that experience, I was just focused on trying to figure out how to maintain myself and my integrity."

When Flora graduated she set up a practice that reflected her values in treating patients and in working with her employees. She has been determined to create different types of relationships, relationships not based on the physician having the power, but based on partnering, whether it be for improved health or a healthy work environment. Her goal was to incorporate complementary medicine and other healing practices for her patients so they would have greater responsibility for their own health.

Flora always challenged the negative power dynamics she saw in relationships, organizations, and in society. Personally and professionally, she rejected inequalities and worked to change how people relate to each other. In her youth she worked at a bank and realized, as a Caucasian, she was offered many more opportunities than her Asian and African-American colleagues. "When it became clear that I was on some sort of a fast track, and that my co-workers who were competent, had more experience, and certainly more desire weren't, I quit. I also wrote a letter saying I couldn't continue working in all good consciousness in a place that had racist policies."

Flora says being an employer has been a learning experience, "I'm trying to create something that is different, because when you think of an employer and an employee there is a relationship and there is power. If the employer has the power, how do you use that power so you are building that person? By building that person you are building a relationship, and by building a relationship you are making the whole enterprise stronger."

She has also worked to create a different type of relationship with patients. "I am so aware that when I go into a room as a physician I have the power. But why? I love it when my patients bring in information and we have a discussion about something, and I have something to add and they have something to add and then a mutual decision is made."

In her medical practice Flora is in awe of the strength and

power she sees in women because of the power of birth. She is deeply moved by women's power of giving life, understanding the ability to have babies gives women a unique type of power and the responsibility to make choices. She is committed to helping women have their own power through controlling their own bodies. "How do women find their power? By being true to themselves, by expressing themselves, by starting to question and taking control of their lives. For me, the whole question of women being able to control their lives is tied to what they do with their bodies. And if you take that away from a woman, to me that is going right at the heart of women being able to have power."

Chava ✕ Happening from Her

"I think when I reflect on the whole courage thing I get tripped up with the definition. I'm not sure I'm courageous when it never occurred to me that I can fail. If it never occurs to you that you might fall off the cliff—what is brave?"

While it never occurred to Chava that she wouldn't become a rabbi, it has taken a strong belief in her own power to make it a reality. From an early age, Chava had a sense she had the power to create her experiences.

She was less than four years old when her baby brother died of a heart disorder. During his illness and death she had a lot of solitude as her parents struggled to cope with their grief. "I was very alone and it felt like the whole world fell apart." The night he died Chava was visited by the prophet Elijah who comforted her. He told her it was ok to be sad about missing her brother, but that he was fine. "I knew then I had a choice of how I was going to grieve his death." Elijah also told her she was to become a rabbi, something that, at the time, women simply didn't do.

Chava's life has required her to tap into her courage and sense of power. Rather than staying in the traditional Jewish denomination she was raised in, she chose a smaller, lesser known seminary for her basic studies. Then she moved on to an even more radical school for her ordination. Finally, she chose to settle in a small Midwestern resort town to begin her career. "When we began our synagogue many people in the community said we'd be lucky to get ten people. It never occurred to me it wouldn't work."

Eight years later it has worked. Now the leader of a thriving congregation, Chava is faced with the new challenges of putting in place the structure and elements needed so the organization will grown and live beyond her. "There is a lot of letting go in this process which is both wonderful and a little bit scary. There's an egolessness to cultivate and our egos don't really want to do that, so it's difficult." Chava says she is determined to usher in the changes needed for the sustainability of the congregation so it will be there for future generations long after she's gone.

Chava would like some time to create a family. After losing the pregnancy of several invitro fertilization attempts, Chava and her husband are courageously redefining and reconsidering what it means to have a family. One evening while watching a movie where the couple has a baby at the end of the story, they found themselves sitting on the couch holding hands and weeping. "We were in that type of grief where everything was about everyone else having a baby, when my husband turned to me and said, 'I don't want to lose you to despair.' I realized then that even in this situation we still have to choose life and happiness to not become bitter." Chava is proud of the fact that through the entire experience she kept teaching and tutoring the children of her congregation. "There are times when it is hard and I have a sense of wanting to pull away and isolate myself. It's a daily choice to say I will go where there is pain and not become bitter."

For Chava it all comes down to remembering she has the power "to have life happen from her" that keeps her moving forward. "I want to come from a place of higher consciousness, the day-to-day acts of putting colors on the palette that makes a cohesive set of conscious choices."

Elizabeth ✗ A Warrior's Heart

When you meet Elizabeth you are greeted immediately with a quiet strength that seems unshakeable. Her open heart is so inviting it is difficult to believe that it has witnessed great sorrow. Elizabeth knows the courage it takes to live with a warrior's tender heart.

"I'm very comfortable talking about those times in my life when I just about lost it. My divorce is probably one of the best examples. It was just one of those times when everything about who you thought you were, you no longer were."

For Elizabeth, divorce was particularly complicated. Not only did she have her children to consider, but she had also co-founded her business with her husband. "The workplace became very challenging as my ex-husband and I were now at odds in our perception of power, money, and the organization. And there were so many conflicting forces within me and in the culture. I had a lot of shame, pain, and grief around not being an intact family, and being a single mother created lots of worry about money. I had to just keep listening to my own heart and not the other voices."

In Elizabeth's life it has been times like these when she

tapped into her courageous heart. She used these experiences as fertile ground for soulful searching and her own spiritual work. "I have used the big difficult times and even the smaller challenging events to break open instead of break down."

Today Elizabeth feels like her life is exploding as the seeds she has sown in her business and family life are coming to fruition. "I feel ever more connected to the idea that my own life and my perceptions of reality are enough and valid and necessary. My early years, especially being a young person in business, I was much less confident about the validity of my voice. I would be in board meetings with all men and I would want to voice what had meaning to me—like how our staff was feeling or if we were walking our talk—and it seemed that no one would listen. I did not understand why."

The more challenged Elizabeth felt, the more she resorted to a defense mode that came across as weepy or attacking. Then she would berate herself internally for not being able to play the game. "It wasn't until I began to understand that *my* truth was part of *the* truth, and not something less than valid, that things began to change. I began to see that I, as a woman, hold a part of the truth that the world desperately needs." The clearer Elizabeth became about the validity of her approach to business, the more she was able to guide the organization with "the scent of preservation, care, love, and inclusion" that is native to women.

As Elizabeth grew to accept and appreciate her feminine approach she found herself growing into a leader with a warrior's heart. One of her teachers, a Tibetan master says, "A warrior's heart is a tender heart, one that feels the sorrow and the joy. It is where true power comes from."

It took that true power and a hefty dose of courage for Elizabeth to lead her organization through a recent period of change. "Every big move that I have made at work, when I have stood for what I believed, especially if it is different from what others believe, has taken a lot of courage. As women, we often want to be liked above all. But sometimes it is more important to lead than to be liked. To show that because I am a leader the buck stops here—that has always and continues to take courage."

Elizabeth says she credits her biggest companion—meditation—with providing the means for staying centered. When she feels herself shutting down and becoming hyper-reactive, judgmental, and uninclusive, she knows it's time to strike the meditative pose. "Even the posture with my strong, straight backbone forces my chest and my heart open so I can counter my reactivity with openness." This posture has become a metaphor for Elizabeth's approach to living a powerful and courageous life.

"Courage to me is the ability to be exactly who you are at every moment—to show up fully in the fire and take a stand, but not in a rigid way. It's about staying open to the other person's point of view and to always remember that you know just a piece of the answer, and the other person will fill in the holes for you, if you include them."

Barbara M.H. ✕ Evolutionary Pioneer

Barbara has long known her purpose is in changing the world and helping others understand their power as evolutionary pioneers. At seventy-five years old she continues to guide women and men in their transition to the next stage of evolution.

She grew up in a time when there was no women's movement and little support for women to develop an identity apart from being a wife and mother. Like many women of her generation Barbara married in her twenties and started having babies. While she loved her husband and children deeply she realized she felt a stirring to express herself beyond her family identity. "I was some unknown creature inside myself, pulsing internally to express its self, but I had no idea what to do. I found that when I was pregnant and nursing I would be relieved from the drive for self-evolution as I became immersed in the drive for self-reproduction." Finally, after her fifth child, her depression was so great Barbara couldn't ignore her frustration and yearning any longer. "I felt like I was a woman of stone and then I heard an inner voice for the first time that said, *I won't let you die.* Once I heard that voice I began to get in touch with my authentic self. Out of the pit of despair that came from a trapped identity with no models, no tools, and no guidance, I cultivated my authentic self by inner listening, journal writing, and reading. I am an example of someone who was compelled to understand why I was on this Earth."

Barbara says she realized her life purpose was to express and work with others to understand humankind's evolutionary potential, i.e., the power of individuals to affect, control, and change the evolution of life on Earth. Her concept of conscious evolution is based on her belief that all humans on the planet are connected in our power to create a positive future. She believes that we are "born as co-creative, co-evolving humanity and we must improve our ability to use our powers ethically, effectively and consciously to achieve a positive future." Barbara sees that women are in the midst of becoming feminine co-creators and much of her work is "to understand, incarnate, and model in all humility who we are becoming." She realizes that her purpose is, in essence, a prime vocation. She says, "A prime vocation is an innate calling that you never could have made up yourself. It is not a good job, a good profession, or even a goal. It is a life pulse."

Once she tapped into her passion to understand and communicate humanity's evolutionary potential, Barbara's life changed. "There is a tendency to self-suppress in order not to lose those who love us, so the courage is to risk relationships by expressing your full creativity. You can take the risk of expressing yourself without having to break up the relationships you love if you communicate and if your spouse or partner is also willing to grow." In Barbara's case, when she did express herself and her deep sense of purpose it resulted in divorce and created what she calls her second motherhood. "In my first motherhood I mothered my five children, and in my second motherhood I was mothering my self and my own work in the world. I, of course, included my children in it, but I became aware I had a Self to express and a life purpose I had to mother like I had mothered the children." She learned she could move mountains by taking a stand and finally getting over her feminine desire to please.

In reflecting on the need for women to know and express their authentic Self, Barbara believes, "Our own self-development and self-expression are vital requirements for the future of all our children. Instead of thinking of yourself as self-centered for doing it, you have to put the value of yourself in the world because without you and me and each of us, we are not going to make it. The children will not make it. Also, if you, as a woman, start to grow, everyone around you will also grow; they will be inspired by you. Out of my five children, five out of five have strong life purposes. We all support each other in fulfilling our life purposes."

Intensely motivated to fulfill her purpose, Barbara has achieved much in her life—and often in very visible, public ways. Despite her many accomplishments she wrestles with self doubts. "I think everyone has original toxic thoughts—mine is that I am a failure. I have a very big vision, but sometimes I think, *Barbara, you haven't achieved anything like your potential,* and it will literally feel as though there is a knife in my heart. I would call that the closest to the devil as I have ever felt. When I feel I am a failure it constricts my heart and I become self-judgmental. It's very destructive." When asked how she copes with her self-doubts, she offers, "The best thing I can do is to communicate with at least one other person and to share my feelings with somebody I love—somebody who recognizes and knows the true me. Also, I shift my attention to my essential self and recognize that my sense of failure comes from my wounded child speaking. So, I comfort it—I don't hit it over the head, but I become maternal to that self."

Barbara takes her role as an elder seriously in pointing the way to other women in becoming what she describes as "evolutionary pioneers." She says, "I think it is extremely important that we have models of who we are becoming. A woman's greatest power is the discovery of the authentic self that is her own essence, and then the deeper discovery of how she will express what she was born to do. When a woman starts to rise up with her deeper life purpose she finds herself at the edge of evolution because she does not want to fit into the existing culture. The women of power today become pioneering women again, not on the physical frontier, but the spiritual and social frontier. As an elder, my purpose is to model this evolutionary change for other women; it is not my role as an elder to tell you about the past, but to stand at the horizon and tell you what is coming."

✕ Afterword

THE STORIES WE INCLUDED in this book were intended to be a foundation for expanding our understanding about how women view their courage, and the many ways they are redefining their power. Every interview was a gift—to us. Every interview was an opportunity for us to look at these concepts with new lenses.

In the course of doing the interviews every woman we spoke with told us that, as a result of talking about their lives they felt stronger, prouder... bigger. The process of sharing their stories helped them remember what they had forgotten—their innate self-determination, their deep power, and their everyday courage that carried them through tragedies and triumphs.

Ultimately, however, it's *your* story that is important. We know you have unique tales to tell of how courage has shown up in your life. Times when you've made the choice to live with self-determination. How you've tapped into wellsprings of your power. How you've changed the world   your world   for the better.

It's time to acknowledge, honor, and celebrate the many ways you have and are now creating your own Courage Code.

Biographies

✕

Barbara

Barbara Hill is President and CEO of the Michigan Women's Foundation, the first philanthropic enterprise of its kind in the state, and the only one designed specifically for women and girls. Prior to her current position she was a volunteer for nine years with the Foundation, serving on the Board of Trustees and as a member of several key committees. A self-described feminist, Barbara has 25 years of local and national experience with programming, philanthropy, and advocacy for women's issues. She has previous experience with the Girl Scouts of the USA and YMCA of the USA, and served as a consultant with the $100 million Detroit Empowerment Zone Development Corporation. Barbara lives in Detroit with her husband. She enjoys cooking and creating recipes. She is new to gardening, but already is getting requests from neighbors to design their flower beds with color and flair. Barbara likes old movies and classical music, and considers herself a real homebody.

Barbara M.H.

Barbara Marx Hubbard is President of the Foundation for Conscious Evolution. She also served as co-founding Director of the World Future Society and of the Association for New Thought. Her books include The Hunger of Eve, The Evolutionary Journey, *and her latest,* Conscious Evolution, The Great Awakening: A Spirit-Motivated Plan of Action for the 21st Century. *In 1984, Barbara made history when her name was placed in nomination for the Vice Presidency of the United States. Her passion is her work because it keeps drawing forth more life and creativity, and connects her to people worldwide. Barbara has five children and eight grandchildren, and lives in Santa Barbara, California with her beloved life partner/soul mate.*

Bethany

Bethany Piziks, DDS, is a dentist and owner of Cadillac Family Dental Care. She graduated from dental school in 1994 and started her own practice two years later. Bethany's state-of-the art dental office provides complete, comprehensive dental care and maintains a focus of serving clients in a high quality, innovative, team-oriented manner. She currently lives in Cadillac, Michigan with her spouse and 10-year-old son. Bethany has one horse, one dog, and three cats and she loves them all. She enjoys the outdoors in any season and takes joy in staying in shape. Softball is her favorite sport and she plays in many tournaments throughout the summer. She's passionate about helping others live better lives, whether by fixing their smile or offering a listening ear. Bethany's dream is to lead seminars that encourage people to move toward their best possible future of choice.

Betty

Betty Elizabeth Shaw Parsons retired after holding numerous positions with Interlochen Center for the Arts, one of the largest and best-known arts organizations in the U.S., attracting students from around the world. Positions included serving as Head of the Alumni Department, and Editor of Crescendo, The Alumni Magazine. *She was an active volunteer in several organizations—Planned Parenthood, League of Women Voters, and Michigan Art Train. Betty was appointed by Michigan's Governor Milliken to the Michigan Council of Arts, and worked to develop Arts Councils throughout the state. One of her greatest sources of pride was seeing the Councils grow from meetings around kitchen tables to having significant influence in their respective community's growth. Betty raised seven children and now has five grandchildren. Sadly, not long after she was interviewed for this book, Betty became ill and passed away.*

Carol

Carol Navarro, R.N., spent the first half of her nursing career rotating in several different areas of hospital nursing and also worked in home health care. She spent the last ten years in Community Mental Health working with developmentally disabled and mentally ill adults. In the interim between nursing and her committment to returning as a full-time student Carol had her own massage therapy practice for five years. She is now discovering the joy of the parenting transition: she and her husband are proud of their four adolescent children who are evolving into young adults. Carol loves nature and enjoys birdwatching with her six-year-old granddaughter who can easily identify at least eight different bird calls in the field.

Celia

Celia Tomlinson is President and CEO of Rhombus Professional Associates, an engineering firm she founded in 1983. In 1970 she became New Mexico's first registered female professional engineer and in 1983 the first female engineer to serve as a Member in the New Mexico State Board of Registration for Professional Engineers and Land Surveyors. She is the author of Don't Even Tell Me YOU CAN'T. *Celia has received numerous awards including New Mexico's Outstanding Woman and Trailblazer Awards and the Asian Women in Business Entrepreneurial Award. She is a recent widow after being married thirty-five years. She now lives in Albuquerque, New Mexico with her 83-year-old mother and older sister. Celia loves adventure, particularly river cruises, and has traveled extensively. She reads true-crime stories, and has participated in aerobics and yoga throughout her life.*

Charlene

Charlene Proctor, Ph.D., author of Let Your Goddess Grow! *and* The Women's Book of Empowerment, *is founder of The Goddess Network, a live and online self-development venue. She has worked as a simulation architect, researching issues on learning organizations, female leadership, the environment, and corporate spirituality. She is a former board member of the International Simulation and Gaming Association, a worldwide network of academics who study issues of complexity through interactive learning. In addition to being a workshop leader and public presenter, Charlene is a prolific writer of articles, electronic programs, and resources for women who want to discover their inner feminine principles. While deeply committed to helping others along their soul journey, she gains balance in her own life from her husband and two teenage boys. She lives with her family in the Detroit metropolitan area. Her passion is in helping women realize their potential to transform the world through higher levels of conscious awareness.*

Chava

Chava Bahle is the spiritual leader of Congregation Ahavat Shalom in Traverse City, Michigan, as well as the rabbinic director of the Or Tzafon Retreat Center, a center devoted to the study of Jewish mysticism, meditation, and prayer. She received her first smicha (rabbinic ordination) in 1998 from a beth din (rabbinical court) of ordained rabbis. Chava also recently received smicha from the ALEPH Alliance for Jewish Renewal Smicha Program, and continues her studies as she trains more deeply to become a maggid, an inspired teacher on the path of life. Chava teaches courses in religion, spirituality, writing, and nonprofit leadership at Northwestern Michigan College, where she helped found the nonprofit leadership certificate program. She was a volunteer chaplain for the Michigan Department of Corrections for 18 years, and was the 1999 recipient of the City of Traverse City's Sara Hardy Humanitarian Award for her work in human rights. She has also been recognized by the Michigan Department of Civil Rights for her leadership. Chava lives in Suttons Bay, Michigan with her husband and cat, Midrash.

Christie

Christie Minervini is the owner of Gallery Fifty, an art gallery featuring unusual jewelry, functional art, and fine craft from over seventy-five North American artists. Prior to opening her business, she was a sales and marketing professional with Traverse, Northern Michigan's Magazine. *She also was an owner of Watermark Image Resource, an advertising agency specializing in not-for-profit marketing and special events, and Executive Director of St. Joseph Today, a nonprofit membership-based promotional organization. Christie currently lives on Old Mission Peninsula in Traverse City, Michigan, and is looking forward to moving into a condominium at the old Traverse City State Hospital which her husband's family is redeveloping. Her daughter is her passion and daily companion. Christie creates beaded jewelry and has been honing her metalsmithing skills to create a wholesale line of jewelry for sale in galleries nationwide. Film and travel are her favorite pastimes.*

Deb

Deb Wyatt Fellows began Traverse, Northern Michigan's Magazine *in her early twenties, and twenty-five years later her prospering company,* Prism Publications, Inc., *also publishes* Northern Home & Cottage, Destination Northern Michigan *and* Meetings North. *Last spring she wrote and published the first of what she hopes to be many books,* Reflections on a Life Up North. *Deb has served on numerous community boards and commissions, was a founding board member of the Grand Traverse Regional Land Conservancy, and is currently Vice President of the Leelanau Land Conservancy. She lives in Leelanau County in Northern Michigan with her husband and four children.*

Debbie

Debbie Stabenow is a U.S. Senator who made history in 2000 when she became the first woman from Michigan elected to the U.S. Senate. In November 2004 she was elected by her colleagues to be the third ranking Democrat in the Senate as Secretary of the Democratic caucus—an unprecedented honor for a freshman Senator. She serves on several Senate committees including Budget, and Special Committee on Aging, and was named head of the Senate Health Care Task Force for her Caucus in the last Congress. During her time in the U.S. Senate, Debbie has championed efforts to protect the environment, consumers, seniors, children and families. Debbie is only the second person from Michigan to have served in both houses of the Michigan State Legislature and in both houses of the U.S. Congress. Her home is in Lansing, Michigan where she lives with her husband. She has three grown children. Debbie loves music and considers Barbara Streisland and Bonnie Raitt her favorite performers.

Debby

Debby Werthmann is a certified Life Coach through Martha Beck's North Star Life Coach Training. She counsels and mentors women going through midlife issues, such as transition, caretaking, over-whelm, problematic relationships, divorce, and empty nesting. Her work allows her to act on her passion to help women make healthy choices, turn around negative perceptions, self-belittling talk and actions that hold them back from moving forward. She previously worked for Clinique, Christian Dior, and Lancome in cosmetic sales management and as a make-up artist. Debby lives in Traverse City, Michigan and enjoys spending time with and sharing in others' lives. She loves traveling, kayaking, walking on the beach and in the woods, swimming, reading, cooking, quilting, and good dark chocolate.

Elizabeth

Elizabeth Lesser is the Cofounder and Senior Advisor for Omega Institute, the largest adult education center focusing on health, wellness, spirituality, and creativity in the U.S. She is the author of The Seeker's Guide: Making Your Life a Spiritual Adventure *(formerly titled:* The New American Spirituality: A Seeker's Guide) *and* Broken Open: How Difficult Times Can Help Us Grow. *For more than 25 years, Elizabeth has studied and worked with some of the leading preeminent thinkers and practitioners in the fields of healing and spiritual development. She has also written for national magazines and websites. She has been interviewed on radio, appearing on nationwide shows including NPR's "All Things Considered" and "To the Best of Our Knowledge." Television appearances include CNN and Wisdom Television. Previous to her work at Omega, she was a midwife and childbirth educator. She has been active in local environmental issues for the past 20 years.*

Eva

Eva Petoskey has over 25 years of experience working with tribal communities throughout the Great Lakes region on issues related to wellness, education, evaluation, and cultural preservation. For the past 15 years she has operated a consulting business specializing in community-based research and evaluation services for tribes and Indian organizations. Eva has Bachelor and Master's degrees in Education, and has completed coursework for a Doctorate in Educational Administration, Research, and Public Policy. She is a member of the Grand Traverse Band of Ottawa and Chippewa Indians and served on the Tribal Council for six years. She is the author of numerous articles related to engaging communities in change and valuation. Eva lives in Peshawbestown, Michigan with her husband of 17 years, children ages 11 and 14, and two wonderful yellow labs. She loves gardening, watching and listening to birds, writing poetry, telling stories, and practicing meditation. She is passionate about many things, including healing the human heart and all things in nature.

Evelyn

*Evelyn Dilsaver is Executive Vice President for Charles Schwab & Co.,
President and CEO for Charles Schwab Investment Management, and
a member of the Executive Committee at Charles Schwab. She has
responsibility for the $145 billion proprietary mutual fund business, the
12th largest mutual funds in terms of assets in the U.S. and insurance
and annuities. Prior to Schwab she was a controller for a bank, and a
senior manager for a big four public accounting firm. Evelyn also serves
as Chair of the Board for Women's Initiative for Self-Employment in
San Francisco, California. She lives in the San Francisco Bay Area and
has been married to her high school boyfriend for 27 years. Evelyn has
three boys, ages 14-21, and a cat who thinks it is a dog. She plays volleyball, is an avid crossword puzzler and knitter, works out with
weights and fast walking, and loves adventure vacations.*

Flora

Flora Biancalana, MD, is a Family Practice Physician in Traverse City, Michigan. Her practice, Rising Star Wellness Center, focuses on providing options to improve health and well being in a holistic manner. She also serves as the Medical Director for the Community Health Clinic, a free clinic serving low-income patients. Flora was a Resident Physician for the Grand Traverse Band of Ottawa and Chippewa Indians. Prior to being in the health field Flora was a community organizer, veterinary technician, waitress, bookkeeper, security guard, and milked cows on a dairy farm. She currently resides in Northern Michigan on 40 beautiful acres of trees and plants with her life partner, two dogs, and five cats. She enjoys travel and has been to Central America, Italy, and Peru. Flora loves to cook, garden, dance, explore the plant world, especially herbs, and has a passion for simplicity.

Geri

Geri Larkin, P'arang, is the author of numerous books on Buddhism,
including Stumbling Toward Enlightenment, Building a Business
the Buddhist Way, *and* First You Shave Your Head. *Until recently,*
when she embarked on a Buddhist pilgrimage, she was The Guiding
Teacher for Still Point, a Zen Buddhist Temple in Detroit, Michigan.
Still Point is a community of Zen practitioners committed to awakening
hearts of great wisdom and compassion and offers retreats, workshops,
and meditation services. P'arang spent three years in the Maitreya
Buddhist Seminary prior to her ordination in 1995, one of few women
monks. Her teacher was Venerable Samu Sunim, a Korean Zen Master
who started several Buddhist Temples in North America, including the
Zen Buddhist temple in Ann Arbor, Michigan where P'arang was a
dharma teacher before founding Still Point. She has served on Michigan
Governor Blanchard's communication staff and had a successful career
as a management consultant.

Gretchen

Gretchen Ulhlinger has devoted her professional energies for the past 22 years toward the development of an authentic Montessori school for families. She began as classroom teacher/administrator and is now Head of School for the Grand Traverse Montessori School. Recently Gretchen helped the school complete a $4.5 million building project on an 8-acre campus. She and her husband of four years live in a historic district in Traverse City, Michigan with two cats and one dog. Gretchen is passionate about her two grown daughters who are vibrant young women earnestly pursuing their own professions. Her gardens bring her great joy, and she is both soothed and stimulated by the ever-changing waters of the Great Lakes. In the winter she cross-country and downhill skis. She is committed to her work and spends a great deal of time pursuing knowledge and wisdom about human develop-ment. Gretchen enjoys travel, reading, and lingering in art galleries and museums. She is an enthusiastic audience of music concerts, opera, readings, and theatre.

Jill

Jill Warren, A.B.D. is Senior Consultant for Grant Development Services with Metasoft, Inc. in British Columbia, advising clients around the world on governance, development, and strategic planning. She previously was Executive Director and CEO of Planned Parenthood in Northern Michigan. Jill has a Master's degree in Public Administration and is a doctoral candidate in Family and Child Ecology focusing on child maltreatment prevention and public policy. She has taught accounting, management, and human ecology classes at numerous Midwestern colleges and universities. Jill lives with her husband, dog, and cat in a church parsonage in Vancouver, BC. She is very proud of her strong, confident grown daughter, and is passionate about social justice, reproductive rights, teaching, and entertaining and decorating for the holidays. Jill enjoys reading social-action and progressive news; her guilty pleasure is reading home decorating magazines.

Joanna

Joanna Lauber is a certified Social Worker with the State of Michigan.
Since 1978 she has been a counselor in private practice serving clients
with a holistic approach, incorporating hypnosis, meditation, and
energy work. Five years ago she moved to a resort community in
Northern Michigan, and began working part-time from her office in
Traverse City, Michigan and part-time from her home office. She has
been involved as an activist with Traverse City for Peace and in historic
preservation for her small town. One of her favorite projects has been
expanding her township library. Joanna practices meditation regularly,
and loves doing ceramics, hiking, walking on the beach, and kayaking.
She lives in an old, historic home with her cat, Tigger, and black lab,
Clarabell, who goes to work with Joanna.

 Judy

Judy McCorkle is currently Senior Estate and Financial Planner for Financial Investment and Management (FIM) Group, a fee-only wealth management organization with offices in Hawaii, Wisconsin, and Michigan. She has been actively involved in estate and financial planning, probate, trust administration, and investment management since 1980. She is a Certified Financial Planner (CFP), and a Certified Trust and Financial Advisor (CTFA). Prior to joining FIM Group, Judy served for twelve years as Assistant Vice President of First Hawaiian Bank's Assets Management Division for the Island of Maui. Judy participated in the Peace Corps training program on Hawaii's Big Island, and served as a Peace Corps Volunteer in the Ulithi Atoll of the Yap District. She also managed a documentation center for the United Nations in Gabon, West Africa. Judy and her husband are residents of Maui.

Julie

Julie Abrams is the Executive Director of the Women's Initiative for Self Employment in San Francisco, California, an organization assisting low-income women of diverse ethnic and social backgrounds in becoming economically self-sufficient through entrepreneurial activities. Currently she also serves on the boards of La Clinica, a community health clinic system, and CAMEO, the California Association for MicroEnterprise Organizations. Previously, Julie was the Deputy Director and Development Director of the Merit School of Music in Chicago. She has been married for 13 years to her husband, Raul, who, she says, does not compete with her—he just loves and supports her on their partnership path. Julie has two terrific children, ages 12 and 9. She likes to hike the mountain behind her house, kayak on the Bolinas lagoon and spend time with her family. She speaks Spanish fluently, and loves being surrounded by nature and children.

Karen

Karen Sterk is the Director of the Uptown and Downtown YWCA Health and Fitness facilities in Minneapolis, Minnesota and provides direction for the Women's Wellness Program. Prior to that she held numerous leadership positions in fitness organizations, gaining experience in women's fitness and fitness for clients at-risk due to health conditions, obesity, etc. Early in her career she was the first female Recreation Director for a men's prison in Michigan, as well as launching her own health and fitness business for women of all ages. Her unique approach to addressing the needs of women —mind, body, spirit —earned her the first Tribute! Award in Fitness given by the YWCA in Grand Rapids, Michigan. Karen holds a Master's degree in Exercise Physiology. She is married and has two highly creative, passionate daughters. Karen loves to travel and recently has become addicted to hot yoga.

Kate

Kate Noone is currently Vice President for Davenport University's Online and International Programs. She has served in a variety of capacities with Davenport, including Campus Executive Director and Director of the Learning Academy. Kate began her venture into college administration as an instructor and Department Chair for a college in Western Michigan, after working in nonprofit organizations such as Salvation Army and YWCA Domestic Crisis Center. She has a Masters in Business Management and is currently working to complete a certificate in Health Care Administration. She frequently visits her grown daughter in Florida, and loves spending time on the beaches of Lake Michigan.

Laura

Laura Oblinger is the Senior Vice President of the Traverse Area
Chamber of Commerce, the 3rd largest Chamber in Michigan. She
serves as Executive Director of the Chamber Foundation's Leadership
Grand Traverse Program. She is an experienced professional in the field
of marketing, advertising, public relations, and business development,
and received her Bachelor's degree in Marketing. Laura also serves as a
Board of Trustee for her alma mater, Davenport University, as well as
for GTP Industries and Junior Achievement. She is a native of the
Traverse City, Michigan area and shares an active life with her hus-
band embracing the beauty the region has to offer. Laura loves to kayak
and she is looking forward to taking her new baby daughter with her
as soon as possible.

Lisa

Lisa Franseen is in private practice as a psychologist providing therapy for teens and adults with a holistic and earth-based healing approach. She specializes in ecological psychology and offers college courses, writes articles for local independent newspapers, and co-facilitates workshops helping to cultivate a sense of interconnectedness and empowerment to the earth. Prior to moving to Northern Michigan to be closer to her family, Lisa lived in Colorado where she had a private practice, led women's empowerment and wilderness trips, guided canoe trips down the Colorado River, and conducted "Earth Walks" to help others hear the voice of the earth. She currently lives outside Traverse City, Michigan in a "green" log home in the woods with her partner, snowshoes, and mountain bike. Lisa's passions include all natural places outdoors, gardening, the study of Buddhism, and learning to live as simply and sustainably as she can. She came to Michigan via a year-long worldwide pilgrimage for self-exploration and discovery.

Lynda

Lynda Wonn is presently the Vice President for Campus Operations at Davenport University's campus in Dearborn, Michigan, and was formerly the Academic Dean for this campus. She has a Master's degree in Public Administration. Her venture into higher education was preceded by over 20 years in health care, mostly in nursing administration. She previously worked for the Peer Review Organization for the State of Michigan and was responsible for overseeing the quality of health care rendered to Medicare and Medicaid beneficiaries for 79 of Michigan's 84 counties. A self-described "dabbler," Lynda likes to explore many things. Currently she enjoys sailing and has a sunfish sailboat to practice on. She also likes music, cooking, and growing herbs. She is an avid reader, especially of mystery novels and is addicted to books-on-tape.

Lynn

Lynn Larson is retired and hopes to stay that way in order to follow her passions of political activism, travel, and occasional teaching stints in exotic places. She serves as the Chairperson of the Grand Traverse Democratic Party. She is past Vice President of the Michigan Education Association, and previously taught high school for many years. Lynn lives outside Traverse City, Michigan on a lake with her cat, Oreo, significant other, and occasional family members. Her hobbies include traveling to out-of-the-way places—she has been to 52 countries and islands, doing her own wandering. She has five fabulous grandchildren and has made it a practice to take each one, when they turn 13 years old, alone on a trip of their choice. Lynn is a reader, a lover of card games, a knitter, a swimmer and a snorkeler. She enjoys all weird and good food, and meeting people in all parts of the world.

 Marilyn

*Reverend Dr. Marilyn Sewell is in her fourteenth year as Senior
Minister of the First Unitarian Church of Portland, Oregon. She is
also a writer/editor, having published five books, the last of which is
an anthology of personal essays entitled,* Breaking Free: Women of
Spirit at Midlife and Beyond, *which explores spiritual deepening in
women as they age. Marilyn recently received an Honorary Doctor of
Divinity degree, and was also awarded the A. Powell Davies Preaching
Fellow, Excellence in Preaching Award. She is a much sought-after
speaker on spirituality, justice, environmental ethics, fair trade, and
women's issues. Marilyn has two grown sons, and one five-year-old
grandson. Her cat, Molly, keeps her company in her home in a historic
district of Portland, and in her spare time she enjoys meals with friends
and good films.*

Marsha

Marsha Smith has served since 1997 as the Executive Director of Rotary Charities of Traverse City, an organization that has awarded over 500 grants totaling approximately $30,400,000 since its inception. Its funding priorities are affordable housing, education, environment, culture, and strengthening families. Previously she served as Executive Director of the Grand Traverse Regional Community Foundation. Marsha has a wide range of community interests and has held a variety of leadership roles in environment, growth management, cultural, educational, and health organizations. She is married and has one grown son. She enjoys cycling, sailing, kayaking, camping, and reading. She was recently part of a three-woman team that won first place in the Manistee Sports Fisherman Association's Ladies Classic Fishing Tournament.

Mary

Mary O'Connor, M.A., M.S.W., C.S.W., is a retired teacher with a Master's degree in Early Childhood. After twenty-eight years as an inner-city primary grade teacher, she earned a Master's degree in Social Work. Mary has worked in areas of domestic violence, addiction, and mental health. She has been active in the development of Miracle Manor, a unique, innovative program for addicted women and their children. She serves on the Michigan State Board of Social Work and on the Disciplinary Sub-Committee of the Board. For seven years she has been a Human Rights Commissioner for the City of Traverse City. Mary lives with her husband of 36 years in a wonderful Victorian home, and has four grown children and one very special granddaughter. She is a big reader and lover of books of all kind, and has a cottage in Canada she and her family enjoy. Mary loves antiques and enjoys taking a discarded or used-up piece of the past and bringing it back to life.

Mary W.S.

Mary Waddell Sutherland, M.A., has a long and illustrious career as a communication consultant and trainer. She received her Bachelor's degree in 1952 from Ohio State University in speech education and her Master's degree in communication arts, with a major in knowledge utilization with cognate in women's studies from Michigan State University in 1974. She was in private practice as a counselor for the Bay Area Psychiatric Clinic in Northern Michigan, and was a widely sought after speaker and instructor on topics of assertive behavior and women's behavior. Her reputation as a public speaker led to her selection as a member of the National Speakers Association. Mary was named Outstanding Woman of the Year in 1981 by the Traverse City Chapter of Zonta International. She was twice selected to be included in Who's Who of American Women. She is the author of Claim Your Self *and co-authored* Mommy and Daddy's Book of Games, Rhymes and Finger Plays. *She was also a prolific writer for the Detroit News. Mary has six grown children and 11 grandchildren. She loves to travel and participates in Elder Hostels every year.*

Mary Ellen

Mary Ellen Bittner serves as President of Zonta International,
a global service organization of women executives in business and
the professions working together, across political and social bound-
aries, to advance the status of women worldwide. She is also the
Chief Administrative Law Judge for the U.S. Department of Justice,
Drug Enforcement Administration, as well as managing the budget
and supervising the staff of the Office of Administrative Law Judges.
In addition to her juris doctor degree, she holds a Master's degree in
Economics. Mary Ellen has been recognized as a "Woman of Courage
and Leadership" by the Drug Enforcement Administration. She lives
with her husband in suburban Washington, D.C. and has one grown
daughter. Her special interests include programs that help women
achieve self-sufficiency and serving as a volunteer tutor to students
in the District of Columbia Public Schools.

Melanie

*Melanie Herren is founder of the Community Spirit Food Source, Inc,
a nonprofit providing food, clothing, friendship in a dignified manner
to women, children and families experiencing poverty. She is also
employed in the emergency room of Paul Oliver Hospital as an EMT.
One of her passions is to assist women and children experiencing
domestic violence, abuse, and stalking, through public speaking,
personal contacts, and writing. Melanie has traveled around the
country interviewing homeless people as a way of putting a face,
name, and personality to them through her writing and speaking.
She has published poems on the homeless, and recently completed a
short story called "A Gift for Christina," based on her interviews with
a young woman living on the streets of San Francisco. Melanie lives
in Benzie County in Northern Michigan and has two sons, two daugh-
ters-in-law, and two granddaughters, ages five and two. She loves
writing, running with her dog, Maggie, and traveling.*

Nicholeen

Nicholeen Frusti serves as Vice President for The Builders Alliance, a residential general contracting business she jointly owns with her husband. She also works for Northwestern Michigan College as Office Manager and Advertising Manager for the student newspaper, White Pine Press. Nicholeen started college at age 26, and within four years was the President of the Student Government Association and President of Phi Theta Kappa, an International Honors Organization. Out of 1500 nominees, she was chosen as one of twenty students to the All-USA Academic First Team for Community and Junior Colleges sponsored by USA Today. She lives with her husband, three daughters ages 5-11, and sheltie named Annie in Traverse City, Michigan. She loves reading, playing with her daughter, gardening, doing community service, and remodeling her house. Nicholeen's passion is to help others see what they do not see in themselves and her dream is to become a motivational speaker.

Pami

Pami Sprague is keeper of the labyrinth she built in Northern Michigan, named "Walk with Purpose: A Private Sanctuary for Thought and Reflection." She also is a Creative Memories Independent Consultant, co-owner and operator of GBG Painting, and Children's Education Director of Congregation Ahavat Shalom. Pami's professional path has been a wildly eclectic adventure with all roads, at last, leading home. Pami graduated with a Bachelor's degree in Science in 1986. She lives with her husband of nine years, twin six-year-old sons, and cats, C.K. Kitten, Poofy Cat, and Gemini Kitty. Her passions are her sons, keeping the labyrinth, gardening, reading, creating memory albums, hanging out with like-minded/like-hearted people, snowboarding, and snowshoeing.

Patty

Patty Bauer, F.N.P., is a Women's Health Care Nurse Practitioner for Planned Parenthood of Northern Michigan, one of 121 affiliate clinics throughout the country providing high quality, affordable reproductive health care and sexual health information to women, men, and teens. In her role she delivers comprehensive health care, taking time to talk with clients, and encouraging them to ask questions and discuss their feelings in a confidential setting. Patty was previously a Perinatal Outreach Coordinator at a major Medical Center, and a Community Health Nurse. She lives in Traverse City, Michigan with her 15-year-old son, 15-month-old labradoodle dog, and cat, Tansy. Patty has two grown daughters, one in Kansas City, Missouri and one in New York City. She loves to read, kayak, and be in the great-outdoors. Her passion is for her kids.

Patty O.

Patty O'Donnell is the Regional Planner for the Northwest Michigan
Council of Governments, a ten-county regional planning agency.
She is involved in projects throughout the region related to scenic
heritage routes, watershed planning, solid waste, natural hazard
mitigation and sustainable business planning. Previously, Patty was
the Environmental Stewardship Director of the Grand Traverse Band
of Ottawa and Chippewa Indians, and Environmental Education and
Preserve Stewardship Coordinator at the Little Traverse Conservancy
Program. She received the first annual Taimi Lynne Hoag Award for
Environmental Stewardship for the U.S. Environmental Protection
Agency Region 5 Tribal Operations Committee. Patty lives in Northern
Michigan with a partner of 16 years, and Murphy, a beautiful husky
dog who pulls her on her cross-country skis. Her hobbies include bird
watching, handwriting letters to family and friends, cross-country
skiing, reading, walking the dog, nature hikes, and being in Lake
Michigan.

Peggy

*Peggy Krihak is currently working in the public sector as an adminis-
trative assistant in the construction arena following her retirement as
a Staff Sergeant with the Illinois Army National Guard after 27 years of
service. She also serves as the Commander of an American Legion Post.
Previously, she worked in secretarial positions to a CEO and a Senator,
and continues to use the shorthand she learned long ago. She has been
divorced for the last 18 years after 28 years of marriage and leads a full
live involved in the American Legion and other volunteer work. Peggy
is the mother of two daughters and two sons and has tried to instill in
them open-mindedness and good citizenship. She currently lives in
Illinois and tends her garden, reads historical novels, and marches in
parades and to her own tune. One of Peggy's goals is finishing the last
year and a half of her college degree.*

Robin

Robin Long Sanderson is Pastor and teacher of Suttons Bay
Congregational Church, in Suttons Bay, Michigan, and is approaching
her five-year anniversary of her Ordination in the United Church of
Christ. A graduate of Andover Newton Theological School, she previ-
ously was Associate Pastor of the Barrington Congregational Church
in Barrington, Maine. Robin's family includes her husband of five
years, a young son, and three Pembroke Welsh Corgis named Ruby,
Katie, and Willie. She enjoys traveling, reading good fiction, watching
cheesy romantic comedies, quilting, and crafts. Robin's passions are
her family and ministry, progressive politics, and all things Welsh
Corgi.

Sandra

Sandra Ramos founded the first official shelter for battered women in North America in 1970. In 1987 she founded, and still is, Executive Director of Strengthen Our Sisters, a shelter and service program for homeless, battered women and their dependent children in rural New Jersey. It has received recognition for its model programs aimed at breaking the cycle of domestic violence and fostering self-sufficiency. Sandra has received numerous awards, including the 2001 Russ Berrier Top Honor Award for Making a Difference. She has a Master's degree in Applied Urban Anthropology and teaches courses in women's changing roles and dynamics of domestic violence for William Patterson College, and social issues and dynamics of domestic violence at Ramapo College. She lives in a purple Quonset hut that is very nurturing and special. Sandra has two cats, Sappho and Hallow, that follow her as she does a Stations of the Cross Goddess meditation through the woods, putting different energy out for different purposes. She loves to swim, horseback ride, walk, and her passion is fairness and justice.

Sondra

Sondra Shaw Hardy is the founder of the Women's Philanthropy Institute which recently became a program of the Center on Philanthropy at Indiana University. Her award-winning book, Reinventing Fund Raising: Realizing the Potential of Women's Philanthropy, *was published in 1995. Sondra co-writes a fundraising column for the professional bi-monthly journal, "Contributions," and teaches fund-raising courses throughout the country. In 2000 she wrote the handbook,* Creating a Woman's Giving Circle, *and has helped establish women's giving circles nationwide. She is an active volunteer and past President of the Women's Resource Center in Traverse City, Michigan. Sondra loves to read, play golf, travel, spend time with friends, and garden. She has three children and six grandchildren, ages 9–19.*

Suzanne

Suzanne Fraker has worked for the American Medical Association (AMA) for twenty-five years in marketing and communications and is currently Director of Product Development. Suzanne has been President of the Women Health Executives Network, a Board Member of the Illinois Women's Political Caucus, and has published two articles in the "Journal of the American Medical Association" (JAMA). She is certified by the International Mandel Institute, Switzerland, as a Colorpuncture practitioner, certified by the Auro-Soma International Academy of Colour Therapeutics, England, as an Aura-Soma practitioner and is currently completing her course work at the Tama-Do Academy of Sound, Color and Movement. She is a Reiki Master and holds a diploma in therapeutic massage from the Chicago School of Massage Therapy. Suzanne and her husband live in Chicago with their two Bengal leopard cats and a fish. She enjoys biking along the Chicago lakefront, tending to her flower and vegetable container gardens, and is beginning preparations to climb Mount Kilimanjaro in Tanzania, Africa.

Ubaka

Ubaka Hill is a nationally known drummer, teacher, performer, and visual artist. She began drumming professionally at the age of 18 in her home state of New Jersey, and has since performed with various creative artists around the country, and co-founded percussion performance groups. Ubaka is the Founder and Director of the Drumsong Institute, based in Brooklyn, New York, which provides workshops, performances, and related information. She is deeply committed to the emerging tradition of women drummers and is involved in preparing written documentation on the evolving tradition of women and drums in the U.S. Ubaka is editor and publisher of the newsletter "Drumsong/Drumming Womyn's News: Views and Attitudes." She is a shape-shifter, a storyteller, and an innovative drummer in the tradition of jazz and in the spirit of social change.

ж About the Authors

Jennifer & Megan

Jennifer Byron and Megan Raphael met while participating in a three-day, 60-mile Walk for Breast Cancer. Immediately they realized they shared a vision of supporting women in living courageous, fulfilling lives. With that vision they launched the Courage Project.

Jennifer Byron began her career in marketing for the nation's largest privately-held food service distributor where she worked for 14 years before making a bold move to higher education. As an instructor and administrator, Jennifer focused her experiences in nontraditional educational formats for returning adult students, many of them women. She holds a B.A. in Business Administration, M.B.A. in Marketing, M.S. in Communications and is an eager student of learning theory. Jennifer is a licensed Brain Gym® instructor with a background in the field of applied brain research of mind-body integration known as Educational Kinesiology. Jennifer lives in

Traverse City, Michigan, and awakens each day to breathtaking sunrises over the bay and the sounds of a purring cat.

Megan Raphael has over 22 years in organizational development, group facilitation, and leadership training and coaching. For twelve years she was President of Raphael-Leritz Consulting, formerly Raphael Consulting, a successful management development practice in the Pacific Northwest. In addition, Megan has ten years of management experience in health care organizations including Kaiser-Permanente, Oregon Region, and Grand Traverse Band of Ottawa and Chippewa Indians. She has a B.A. in Social Work, and has done M.B.A. course work with advanced courses in organizational development. She is currently completing her certification in coaching through Coach Training Institute (CTI). Megan and her husband, Peter, to whom she has been happily married for over thirty years, live in Traverse City, Michigan, and have two young adult children, Ryan and Alex.

✕ Courage Project

The Courage Project is dedicated to inspiring, informing, and coaching women to courageously create the life they want. Our goals are to:

• Open women's eyes to the strength of their courage and power for living a self-determined life.
• Enliven discussions and stimulate reflection in groups of women for understanding how the feminine face of power can and does change the world.
• Provide a call to action in large numbers of women for changing and bringing greater balance to the world.

Besides publishing The Courage Code, *the Courage Project offers resources including personal and professional coaching, workshops and retreats, and custom-designed keynote presentations and seminars.*

We would love to hear your thoughts about The Courage Code *and/or your personal stories of courage and power. Please contact the authors by email: info@courageproject.com, or phone: 231-922-2234.*

www.courageproject.com